Noo Dan!

Noo Dan!

Douglas C. Smith

The Shetland Times Ltd.
Lerwick
2009

Noo Dan!

ISBN 978 1 904746 45 4

First published by The Shetland Times Ltd., 2009.

Printed and published by
The Shetland Times Ltd.,
Gremista, Lerwick,
Shetland ZE1 0PX.

"The time has come," the Walrus said,
"To talk of many things…"

Lewis Carroll

"Noo dan!" is the Shetlandic version of "Now then!", a bizarre juxtaposition of present and past, which can variously mean any or all of the following: "Hello!"; "What next?"; "I'm glad that's over"; "Where did I put that…?"; "What's your excuse?"; "What have I done?" and more.

CONTENTS

ILLUSTRATIONS

ILLUSTRATIONS

Preface

IN September 2006, Meg was reading the *Saga* magazine, and drew my attention to an article called 'A Life in Words' in which the author describes the surprising rewards in persuading his father to write his memoirs.

"This is something you could do!" was the comment which came my way and, having read the article myself, I decided that I probably could and that I would make a start 'Sometime'.

Time passed and I actually put one or two sheets of ruled A4 into a folder and made a few notes, but nothing serious came of it. Then it struck me that, in actual fact, it might be a good idea (while I can remember) to try to put down on paper some of the things which were happening around me in Lerwick and elsewhere during the past 80+ years, with the primary purpose of leaving a bit of family history which might be of interest to our extended family in the future.

I therefore made a real effort to begin in November 2008, with no idea as to when I may finish, and as time passes more and more things come to mind.

This, then, is dedicated to them, with my blissins!

Should any or all of this appear in book form, let me apologise to anyone who feels aggrieved or offended by anything I have inadvertently written – it was not my intention.

Douglas C. Smith,
Cliff House,
3 Montfield,
Lerwick.

Acknowledgements

MY grateful thanks go firstly to my long-suffering wife for putting up (so far) with my eccentricities during the last fifty-six years, and also to the inventor of this computer programme with the ability to 'cut', 'copy' and 'paste'.

I must also include my good friend, retired headmaster Ian Fraser, for proof reading and sorting out my erring apostrophes and split infinitives.

In the beginning

THE earliest date which I can confirm on the Smith side of the family tree is 12th June, 1763, which was the birthday of Arthur Smith who was born in the house of his father, Andrew, at the Haa of Queyfirth, Northmavine. Arthur was married twice and had thirteen children, all of whom seem to have settled north of Mavis Grind. One of these was my great-grandfather, Arthur Smith, born on 28th August, 1803, at Queyfirth, who moved to Hamar and then to Islesburgh near Mavis Grind, where he was apparently a noted pony breeder and farmer.

In 1830 he married Charlotte Marshall and they had nine children, including my grandfather, Andrew Smith. (Two sons and one daughter left and settled in New Zealand which accounts for the large number of 'Islesburgh Smith' relatives there.) Andrew Smith started work as a shop assistant in the premises of the Inkster family at Brae. The shop and house were in the large stone building on the shore beside the pier where, in those days, all the goods were delivered by sea.

Andrew Smith.

1

Agnes Inkster.

In due course he married the daughter of the house, Agnes Inkster, and they moved to Lerwick where he opened a shop in the premises where the Shetland Times Bookshop now operates. They lived in a flat at 1 Queen's Lane, above the shop, but as the family grew to two boys and five girls the flat was becoming fairly overcrowded and it is said that Granny Smith told her husband it was time that he built her a proper house, so he commissioned the design and construction of Islesburgh House, described as 'a villa', in King Harald Street, and is reputed to have said, "That'll surely sair (satisfy) her."

One of these seven children was my father, Arthur James Smith, born on Christmas Day, 1877. In 1909 he married Grace Brown, daughter of John Brown, a well known entrepreneur and businessman in Lerwick who had extensive interests with land at Freefield, the business premises of John Brown's Herring Curing Company at the foot of Brown's Road, and in fishing. Two of his most successful boats were named after his daughters, Grace and Joey.

Andrew Smith also had land in the docks area, particularly at Garthspool and the Skippadock, so the union of these families was an important one in business terms. When John Brown died, his businesses should have passed down to his son, but he had been killed during the First World War so the assets were divided between the two sons-in-law, and my father inherited the curing business, later to be called the Anglo-Scottish Herring Curing Company.

Islesburgh House.

In the meantime, Arthur James Smith and Grace Brown had produced a family of two boys, Andrew John (nicknamed 'Bay') in 1910, and Arthur James Junior in 1913. Their father was a captain in the Gordon Highlanders during the First World War but, when stationed in Aberdeenshire with his family, tragedy struck when his wife Grace died in 1918. The boys, then aged eight and five, came home to Lerwick to be brought up by the aunts, uncle and grandmother in Islesburgh House.

Andrew Smith was a keen businessman and had formed a partnership with a German herring exporter, Max Schultze, with premises in Peterhead and elsewhere. They established the firm of Andrew Smith and Schultze which became well known wherever herring was being cured and exported, the main outlets being Germany and Russia.

Andrew Smith died in 1917 and his business interests passed to his eldest son, Arthur James, with some settlement for his other son, Andrew Wilfred, with, it is said, nothing whatever being left to the females in the family who had to be supported throughout their lives by their brothers.

Articles in the local press in the early 1920s concerning musical performances repeatedly refer to the presence of a regular group of performers including 'Mr Attie Smith' and 'Miss Jennie Campbell'. No doubt

3

Alexander and Mary Campbell, 54 Burgh Road, Lerwick.

this is how they met and became friends and, in 1926, Arthur James Smith married Jean Johnstone Campbell and they set up house at 55 King Harald Street, Lerwick, where they were joined by the two boys, Bay and Jim. This must have been a real wrench for the boys, to have first lost their mother and then to have to leave the house and relatives where they had spent their formative years. I did not appear on the scene for another two years.

So far as the maternal side of my parentage is concerned, the story starts in the Inverness area with my grandfather, Alexander Campbell, born in 1843 at Arderseir, and my grandmother, Mary MacDonald, born in 1863 at Resolis, near Cromarty. He had been a joiner and carpenter involved in the restoration of Ardverikie Castle near Newtonmore, Invernesshire, under the architect Mr Alexander Ross. Mr Ross was then appointed to be architect of Lerwick Town Hall and he took Alexander Campbell with him to be a clerk of works. Whether he and Mary had met before is not known, but she came to Lerwick to join him and they were married in 1885. They set up home at 9 Market Street where their family of six children, including my mother, was born.

After the completion of the Town Hall, Alexander Campbell decided to stay on in Lerwick and was indeed appointed by Lerwick Town Council as the first burgh surveyor under the Burgh (Police) Act, 1892. In this post he was responsible for the health of the inhabitants of the burgh and for the planning, provision, installation and maintenance of infrastructure such as water supply, drainage and roads.

When he was appointed the town was much smaller than it is today. The burgh boundary was at Burgh Road, and between Burgh Road and the Hillhead there was a grassy valley, the only intervening roadway being High Street, which ran from the Lower Hillhead to the foot of Burgh Road. Only one house was ever built on High Street and this was demolished after World War Two, the road itself having vanished long before. In fact, the road called High Street disappeared as part of the development plan for the area between the Hillhead and Burgh Road, which was prepared and supervised by Alexander Campbell. In this plan, St Olaf Street, King Harald Street, King Erik Street, King Haakon Street, Union Street, Harbour Street and so on were laid out and arrangements made for the type of housing to be built there. I have to say that I am still impressed by the foresight which he showed in the openness of the layout of the area of Lerwick where I was born and grew up.

After some time with the Town Council he decided to go on his own and became a very successful architect, designing such buildings as Brentham Place, Brown's Buildings, Carlton Place, 55 and 57 King Harald Street and, coincidentally, at the request of Andrew Smith, Islesburgh House, of which I still have his hand-drawn plans! He also designed and built a house for himself and his family at 54 Burgh Road, as well as several churches throughout Shetland, perhaps the largest of which is at Bigton. Alexander Campbell died in 1924.

So, both my grand-fathers died many years before I was born, but I can still remember Granny Campbell, who died in 1932, as a large rotund lady, perpetually dressed in black and a native Gaelic speaker.

Granny Smith lived on in Islesburgh House with her son and daughters until 1937, and while she was still there I can remember playing hide and seek which was made all the more exciting by the size of the house and the fact that there was a laundry chute from the first floor down to near the kitchen, which was always a great way to escape any pursuers. Those were the days.

Granny Campbell as I remember her.

CHAPTER ONE

This is my story

THE story begins with my birth on 31st March, 1928, in the first floor bedroom of 55 King Harald Street, Lerwick. My mother, born Jean Johnstone Campbell, now the wife of Arthur James Smith, was a small, deceptively frail-looking woman and, because of difficulties anticipated at my arrival there was a nurse present for the event which, fortunately for all concerned, apparently passed off without undue concern.

With Mum, one year old.   *With Dad, 1933.*

7

Reawick, 1930.

Motoring at the Sletts, 1932.

'Fifty-five', as it was always known, is a large semi-detached house at the foot of Cockatoo Brae in Lerwick, built in 1888. (Cockatoo Brae so-called because a previous tenant had possessed a cockatoo which sat in the window and bit chunks out of the window frames, still visible when we occupied the house in 1984.) Relatively large, it is built on four levels, with a double flight of steps up to the front door and steep staircases indoors. It was a very awkward house so far as housework and 'easy-living' was concerned. Because my parents were relatively well-off, in company with many others in similar circumstances we had a maid who did the cooking and cleaning, no easy task in those days before the advent of so-called labour-saving devices. Lighting was by gas lamps, and I can remember as one of my earliest memories the performance of lighting the mantles in the dining-room – I have been told that one of my first sayings was "'ight the gas, pop." Being surrounded by teachers, I also understand that I had an early introduction to the works of Shakespeare, being taught to say, "Out, out, brief candle," when the night-light was extinguished.

Cooking was done on a big black-iron range in the kitchen, although a gas cooker was a later addition. There were coal fires on all floors, and the coal had to be carried from the coal cellar in the basement to all three floors above. Cleaning and dusting was another perpetual chore and another early memory is of the old steam-driven road roller scarifying the then waterbound surface of King Harald Street in preparation for the laying of the tar surface.

I suppose that I had what could be described as a sheltered and favoured upbringing, being the only child in the household. Photographs show that I went on outings and holidays to places like Toab, Reawick, and Stromfirth, usually with my mother and aunts and occasionally joined by my cousin Jean, here on holiday with her mother and father from Surrey. Transport was often by a taxi from Leasks', driven by old Johnnie Leask himself or sometimes by Jimmy.

Dad was involved in the fishing industry as a herring curer and an exporter with premises at Lerwick Fish Market and, during the herring season, in several fishing ports as far apart as Peterhead and Lowestoft. Jim was a member of dad's team and both of them were away from home 'following the herring' for long periods every year. Bay was a banker and left Lerwick in 1933 to work in the Commercial Bank headquarters in London and was only ever briefly back home again. My mother was principal teacher of English at the then Anderson Educational Institute.

Some years (I suppose dependant on the success of the herring fishing) my father would buy a car, a Buick as often as not, to use during the period when he was home, and this would be driven by Sonny Garriock. I can never remember dad at the wheel. There is a story that at the end of one herring season in Lowestoft, he and his partner, Max Schultze, bought a car and set off for Peterhead. Neither, needless to say, had any form of licence or training so when they arrived in York, intending to stay overnight in a hotel, they passed the intended destination and, being unable to reverse, had to circumnavigate the area until they came to a stop at the hotel door.

One rather special holiday took place in 1934. The Norwegian ship *Leda* came to Lerwick on a tour and took some passengers back to Bergen on her return journey. Among these were myself, my mother, and aunts Daisy and Flora. As I recall, we lived in the Hotel Rosenkrantz in Bergen for a week and visited local tourist attractions like the Market, the Bryggen and Mount

On 'Caesar' in the back garden at '55', 1932.

Up Mount Floien, Bergen, Norway, 1934.

Floien. I have a photograph of the waterfall at Steindalsfoss near Norheimsund, so we must have also been there!

Our return was from Bergen to Newcastle on the old ship *Venus*, then farther south to visit my mother's sister, aunt Mary, uncle Alec and cousin Jean at their beautiful house, Glendoone, in a small village called Whyteleafe in Surrey. This was a favourite holiday destination as long as they lived in Whyteleafe, finally retiring to live in Falmouth. Some of my early memories there were seeing a fox in their garden which bordered woodlands, and riding on a Shetland pony in the basement of a big store called Kennards in Croydon. Some years later I can remember being taken to Hendon, then the main London Airport, and seeing the (to me at least) huge biplane airliners 'Horsa' and 'Hengist', and a very early version of the helicopter called an autogiro. These journeys to Whyteleafe, apart from the one via Norway, involved travelling, often by the old yacht-like steamer *St Sunniva*, from Lerwick to Aberdeen, then by 'jiggety-can' steam train to King's Cross, then local train via Croydon and elsewhere to Warlingham station and then car to Glendoone – a real adventure for one so young.

Back home, time for going back to school again was fast approaching, perhaps not the traumatic experience of today for some. Much smaller classes, many friendships already established which would last, and have lasted, for many of us until today, in November 2008, when I am writing this chapter. I will especially mention Douglas Conochie who lived with his parents, brother and sister in the big, imposing property, Braeside, in Law Lane, and Ian Fraser who lived with his parents in a small dark flat in Ogilvie's Buildings, Charlotte Street. Many more friendships followed from across the spectrum of life in the Lerwick of those days and more names will undoubtedly feature as I progress.

It must be remembered that Lerwick was a much smaller town in those days, the burgh boundary still being Burgh Road, and that there were many fishermen and their families from the north-east coast of Scotland and the Moray Firth living in the town in very humble accommodation and fairly impoverished circumstances. Many of the stone-built council houses in the North Road beyond Burgh Road were built for these 'Scotties' as they were known, and one room was actually built as a 'baiting room' where the women folk would sort and bait the long-lines in readiness for the menfolk putting to sea in their small haddock-boats. Having served their purpose, these rooms are now utility rooms or incorporated into the rest of the buildings.

The office of Andrew Smith & Schultze, where my father and brother Jim were ensconced during the herring season, was at the north-east corner of the Albert Building, now the waiting room for the Bressay ferry. This was also my headquarters for the season, and repository for my bike and fishing gear. No fancy rods and reels in those days, just a bit of bamboo cane and some 'scoge', the thin brown line obtainable from Jeemie Irvine's at the head of the pier, now D. & G. Leslie. A packet of sillock and/or piltock hooks and a mackerel scranned from a boat for bait completed the list of necessities. No basket was required and I was told that I once arrived home with my jacket pockets full of sillocks! Fish were teeming at the sides of the piers, sometimes so thick that one could not see the bottom. A real thrill was to catch a mackerel, or even to see the flash of a sea-trout as it sped past. Conger eels lived in holes under the breakwater at the back of the Queen's Hotel, but were reluctant to emerge and be caught. I wonder if anyone catches a 'plucker' these days, and if they still 'smoke'?

A special treat was to 'cadge' a lift for me and my bike on a drifter from the fish market out to Mair's Yard at Holmsgarth and then cycle back to repeat the exercise. One year it was said that I had a 'good fit' (foot) as, just before skipper Robert Duthie set sail for East Anglia on the drifter *Tea Rose* he made me step onboard. He surely thought it was my 'fit' which brought good luck as he had an excellent season and brought me back a big stick of rock with the name 'Yarmouth' all the way through.

Hundreds of drifters from the north-east of Scotland and from East Anglia used to arrive in the harbour at the start of the herring season, landing a sample of their catch at the old fish market building where it was sold to one or other of the many curers. Their premises in my day stretched from the North Ness to the Point of Scatland – Davidson's No.1, Anglo-Scottish, Shearer's, Bremner, Dunbar, Ross, Slater's, Hughes' and many more. Another great event was being at Victoria Pier when the gutters left for the season in East Anglia. Lorries would arrive loaded with their boxes and cases, with the gutters themselves perched on top. There was always some man who arrived late and made a desperate jump from the pier on to the boat as she was pulling away, being hauled aboard by his mates to the cheers of the onlookers onshore.

Hide and seek in the lanes was also great fun. Our boundaries were the Hillhead, Commercial Street, Harbour Street and Queens Lane. These were the days before the lanes were partly demolished and modernised. I wonder how many young folk in Lerwick can differentiate between Pilot Lane and Pirate Lane, or know where Half-Closs stood? The lanes were populated by people living in perpetually dark houses, more-or-less permanently lit by gas or Tilley lamps in the early days, before the advent of electricity, looking across the narrow lanes at another house only a few feet away. There were outside toilets, and water came from stand-pipes, often a large cast-iron thing with the water issuing from the mouth of a lion. The lanes and street were washed on Wednesdays by the chief 'scaffie', Charlie Alger.

One 'dare' was to get from Harbour Street to the Masonic Hall without going on the street or Hillhead. The only really 'dangerous' obstacle was the garden behind the Bank of Scotland, between Bank Lane and Hangcliff Lane, where one was liable to be surprised by, and surprise, the rather irate wife of the banker as she tended her vegetables while we rushed past!

Sometimes there was word of a fight between the Sletts gang and the North Road gang, and it was as well to keep out of the way, not that any bloodshed ever occurred, so far as I am aware, willows being the preferred weapons.

We played football at the 'pitch', a triangle of grass at the south end of King Harald Street. There were a lot of young people in that area and sometimes the so-called playing surface was somewhat overcrowded. The Pottinger, Isbister and Burgess families were joined by Drewie Nicolson, Jeffrey Arthur, Freddy Tait, 'Dinky' Spence, Bertie Robertson, and in due course by 'Maggie Solotti's Army' – Ian Nisbet, John Burgess, Tom Ramsay, and Willie Thompson – a group of boys from country areas who were in lodgings at Mrs Solotti's nearby home. Sometimes the ball would hit the electricity conductors, and an old lady, Mrs Laurenson, who lived in an adjoining house would issue forth claiming that her pans were "jumpin' aff da stove".

CHAPTER TWO

Schooldays

I AM not sure if my case is an isolated one, but I am sure that, from the moment of my birth, my mother's avowed intention was for me to attend university, as she had done, and hopefully qualify in the medical profession. This single-minded approach is, I am sure, just as fraught with problems these days as way back then, being dependent on the totally unknown educational capabilities of the client at the time and also his/her willingness to assimilate the knowledge being offered over the years at school. The outcome for me will be revealed in due course.

For me, getting to school was extremely easy. It was only a few hundred yards from home along the pavements in King Harald Street to the Infant School, and even less to the subsequent Lerwick Central Public School (now the Islesburgh Community Centre). Attendance at the Infant School began in August 1933 with headmistress Miss Anderson. Miss Duncan and the redoubtable Angus sisters, Laura and Chrissie, were the most memorable of the class teachers. No one was allowed out if the weather was unsuitable, and playtimes were spent marching around the pegs in the cloakroom to the piano accompaniment of one of the staff. The only exception to this rule was for 'leave-out' to visit the toilets at the bottom of the playground. Unknown to most people, on the wall of the girls' playground there is a plaque with the Latin inscription *"BYRON, ex canibus, fortissimus et optimus infra jacet. Mori duodec: an: kal: Mar, MDCCCLXVIII"* (*Byron, of dogs the strongest and best lies below. Died 20th March in the year 1868*). No doubt the grave of the cherished pet of a former occupier of the site, possibly even the Latin-speaking headmaster of Hunter's School, built in 1865 on part of the site where the Infant School now stands.

Holding the fort! Bricks for council housing blocks at 110 King Harald Street, 1935. With cousin Jean, the Irvine family, etc.

Then came the first serious move, in August 1935, along the street to the 'Central', as it was known to everyone. The headmaster was W. Robertson Durham, a tall, imposing and threatening figure, whose appearance out of his room on the balcony brought immediate silence – it is said to both pupils and teachers.

I can remember being in the playground when it was announced that Mr Durham had died. Another death which we first learned of in the playground was that of Dennis Watt's father, a lone fisherman who had fallen overboard and drowned somewhere off the Bard of Bressay. Apparently he had been wearing full-length 'flankers' which had filled with water and dragged him down.

Our class numbered 39, the sons and daughters of 'North Road Scotties', bankers, tinkers, a minister, a postman, merchants, farmers – a really cosmopolitan bunch, the survivors of whom have remained firm friends to this day. A few names spring immediately to mind: Ian Fraser, Douglas Conochie, Andrew 'Taity' Watt, Lynn Duncan, Arthur 'Scrap' Mackay, Ian 'Jobson' Mackay, Jeffrey Arthur, 'Snowball' Peterson, 'Tooser' Wiseman, John 'Pottsie' Pottinger, Jack Pottinger, 'Fat Joe' and 'Titch' Mair, Jim 'Hughsie Bird' Hughson, John 'Joker' Welsh, Dennis Jamieson, Hilary Campbell, Peggy Peterson, Betty Manson, Nan Irvine, Sheila Manson, Sheila Cluness, and apologies to the others whose names have not appeared.

The boys from the fishing families in the North Road and Cheyne Crescent areas certainly had a hard life. They usually came from large families and in some instances there was not a sufficient number of shoes to go round and some members came to school in bare feet. There was absolutely no class-consciousness and we went to and from each others houses, depending on what entertainment was on offer. I can remember the Watts having a monkey in a tea-chest in the back green in St Sunniva Street – a very popular destination, but I do not think it survived our climate for long.

In those days stealing was unheard of. I used to leave my bicycle against the wall of '55' King Harald Street, and if it disappeared I knew that one of my 'bikeless' pals would have borrowed it and that it would shortly just as mysteriously re-appear as it would be recognised by all my other pals in any

The 'disappearing' Shetland Star bike, new in 1937.

event. That bike was a 'Shetland Star', assembled and marketed by Johnnie Gear who had a workshop and shop behind the houses at 85 King Harald Street.

A favourite visit to the Conochie home at Braeside was to see a short film of the Schneider trophy on a Pathe projector which stood in the window of the kitchen. In return, when much younger, I had been given a large wooden rocking horse, subsequently named 'Caesar' which had been made in 1857, originally the property of the Cameron family in Bressay, and this was kept in our basement. Many of my pals used to regularly come along to try to get the ends of the bow rockers to touch the low ceiling. 'Caesar' is still going strong, although the bow rockers were replaced some years ago as a safety precaution when there were very small grandchildren in the house.

Sometimes there were special events which were commemorated while we were at the Central. Two of these actually involved 'investitures' where we were all lined up in the respective playgrounds and presented with medals. The first was for the Silver Jubilee of King George V and Queen Mary in 1935 and the second was the Coronation of King George VI and Queen

Me, with 'Scottie', Ian Fraser and Douglas Conochie, King Erik Street, 1937.

Elizabeth in 1937. My only other 'decoration' was a medal from 'Knight's Castille' toothpaste, presumably for brushing my teeth!

School concerts were sometimes performed to commemorate something or other and the triumvirate of Smith, Fraser and Conochie actually were on stage on one occasion to perform a song which went:

"We be three poor mariners, newly come from the sea,
we spend our lives in jeopardy while others live at ease"

Sadly, it never made the charts!

One other outstanding and unforgettable event at the Central took place in room 10, which was situated under the then cookery room. Someone upstairs had knocked over either a heavy table or some other large object and a large part of the ceiling in room 10 suddenly descended upon our heads. This was a heavy plaster ceiling with cornices etc. and the dust and confusion was somewhat disconcerting. Our teacher, Miss Irene Hughson, later the mother of Lord Lamont of Lerwick, immediately did a roll call to check if there were any casualties. Only one boy did not reply, and on checking, this was found to be 'Titch' Mair who was under his desk.

"Are you all right, boy?" asked Miss Hughson, who received the reply, "Please, Miss, a've lost ma pinsill."

Another event which took place when one reached room 10 was the sitting of the 'control exam' by which one was judged capable of progressing on to the Anderson Educational Institute, if one wished, or continuing in the commercial courses at the Central. In my case this took place early in 1940 and with my other successful classmates we should have started at the Institute in August. In the interim, however, war had been declared on 3rd September, 1939. I shall devote a separate chapter to the war years but, in relation to educational matters at the time, some profound changes occurred. The Bruce Hostel for girls was commandeered as the headquarters for the senior naval officer, Admiral the Earl of Cork and Orrery, and the recently completed but never occupied Carnegie Hostel for boys was commandeered for the RAF Operational Signals Headquarters. By this time, Germany had invaded Norway on 9th April, 1940, and mainly because of the very real threat of a German invasion of Shetland from Norway, less than 200 miles away, the start of the autumn session was delayed until 30th September, 1940, and we arrived at the Institute carrying gas masks as well as our schoolbags – no briefcases for pupils in those days!

Being the 'sprogs' we were, of course, subjected to the obligatory 'dookin' in the sinks of the boy's cloakroom by the more senior pupils. I can remember one boy being thrown on to the terrace to the immediate and vocal wrath of our French teacher, Miss Rhoda Hunter, who considered the terrace to be forbidden territory for any pupil and would have dealt severely with the miscreants had she been able to identify them. The victim in question was actually a wartime arrival amongst us, Robert Stewart from Wick, whose father was a major in the army. Being a 'Weeker' (from Wick) he was given the nickname of 'fait', his supposed pronunciation of 'what'. Another notable arrival was 'Rufus', one Roderick MacNeil, the red-headed son of a senior naval officer. Immediately accepted into the clan, these boys enjoyed the camaraderie and excellent education on offer in Shetland.

Our headmaster, Andrew T. Cluness, was a gentle giant, strict and yet caring. The vision of him appearing in the classroom door on a rainy morning with the big timetable board supported on his arm to say, "Class 2, don't come back to school this afternoon," will never fade. Half-days were quite common as there was no transport, no school meals, and even in Lerwick some pupils had a fairly long walk home and back for their lunch. If one made a silly translation in his Latin class he would give a wry smile and say, "Diddums!" His assistant in the Latin department was Chrissie Gray and her lasting immortality is contained in the declension 'acer acris acrae' amended to 'acer a Chrissie Gray'! (At this juncture I must correct the suggestion made in the book published by Dr Bobby Robertson that I was studying Greek. Having discussed this with him we have come to the conclusion that, as I cannot claim to have Greek as one of my linguistic achievements, *ipso facto* he should have said Latin.)

Notable teachers were Rhoda Hunter who ruled the French department with a rod of iron and her assistant, Minnie Anderson; 'Dickie' Dixon, the somewhat eccentric head of science, who seemed impervious to strange gases or acids; Mr Murray and Flora Campbell (my aunt) in the

English department and in the maths department were Bill 'Cheeser' Rhind and John Reid who, if he caught someone talking in class, would say, "If you want to give a speech, get a box and go to the Market Cross – maybe someone will listen to you there!" Art was in the hands of Dorothy Johnson.

Over the years there were obviously changes, but these were relatively minor and we were well taught by the dedicated team who, apart from having to keep us concentrating in spite of the noise of troops and aircraft outside, had to cope with the lack of adequate teaching aids and materials.

One real problem was that the windows in the upstairs classrooms facing the harbour provided a grand view of all the naval activity at the time – and there was considerable activity at that time as the campaign in Narvik in the north of Norway was under way. Many damaged and almost sinking British warships arrived to anchor just below the school to await temporary repairs before proceeding to their bases on the British mainland.

The air-raid shelter for the Institute was in the basement, and from time to time during practices for air-raids, air-raid warden Johnnie Macleod would arrive with a phial of evil smelling liquid which he would drop in through a window whereby an equally evil smelling gas was emitted to test how quickly we could don our gas masks. Classes were often disrupted by air-raid warnings and actual raids, and on one occasion when the senior classes were on their way to the shelter, they claimed that a German pilot waved to them as he flew past down the harbour! Many young Germans had been regularly involved in the herring industry in Lerwick before the war and it was often rumoured that one of these had been recognised as a pilot.

While we were at the Institute a tragic event took place. In November, 1941, a large mine had drifted ashore on the rocky beach to the north of where the torpedo-tubes are built and two naval personnel were attempting to defuse it. Allan Laurenson, a Lerwick-born lieutenant in the RNVR, whose parents lived at Midgarth in Twageos Road, was home on leave and out for a walk at the Knab with his dog. As he was trained in this dangerous trade he decided to offer his assistance. We were in the art room when there was a tremendous explosion and the school was evacuated. It transpired that while they were defusing the mine something happened which caused it to

55 King Harald Street, Lerwick.

explode and the two naval personnel, Allan Laurenson and his red setter dog were blown to smithereens. On our way home round the Knab, Ian Fraser and I were witnesses to some of the carnage caused by the explosion.

Having moved beyond the easy walking distance to the Central School, I was now using my trusty 'Shetland Star' bike for the mile-long journey to the Institute. I often came home via the South End and 'the street', and one afternoon I was making my way past Bain's Beach when something happened which changed my life forever. I found myself lying on the ground outside 'Patter's' butcher shop (later the Citizens' Advice Bureau) with a very sore head and unable to see with my right eye. Thinking that I had been struck by a stone thrown carelessly by someone, I picked myself up and continued home. My mother was very worried, but I had no idea of the consequences until the next day when my right eye was completely bloodshot and I still could see nothing. We went to Dr MacKenzie, who examined me and suggested that I should see a specialist in Aberdeen. Dad arranged for me and my mother to travel down to the Royal Infirmary where we saw a Dr Souter who gave me a very thorough examination. He decided that I had been struck a glancing blow on the side of the eye by some small object which had cut the outer layer and caused bleeding within the eye itself. Consequently, the liquid within the eye, which should have been clear, was now filled with flecks of blood which prevented the light getting to the optic nerve. He said that the flecks might settle to the bottom in time, but unfortunately this was not to be. For about five years I could not see the light from an electric bulb held right before my eye, and I still cannot identify any person or article with my right eye, no matter how close. The only 'bonus' was that my eye was able to be saved, forgoing the need for a glass eye. Only much later did I discover that I had been hit by a pellet from an airgun fired in the vicinity. Although I eventually knew the names of both the culprit, and the owner of the gun (both now deceased), we did not at that era live in times where compensation was the order of the day and my parents did not pursue the matter – what would that have done for my sight?

Instead of the expected six years, we were only at the Institute from September 1940 until Easter 1942. That was when our school was commandeered to be a military hospital and we were to return to the Central, described in an article in the AEI magazine of the time as "A land flowing with milk and Horlicks". The Lerwick Central Public School was, and still is, a large building and, in those days, Institute class sizes were a fraction of what they are today at the Anderson High School. It was therefore decided to split the classrooms in the Central with plasterboard partitions. I cannot imagine that this was a popular solution either with the pupils or teachers, but suffice to say that there was, despite the overcrowding, no undue tension between the two groups of occupants. By and large, the Central pupils continued to occupy the lower floor and the decanted crowd from the Institute were housed on the upper floor. Classes were also held in other buildings such as Islesburgh House, the Methodist Schoolroom and, well remembered, the art classes with Dorothy Johnson in the Albany Hall in St Olaf Street – and pies from 'Bob's'.

Something quite unexpected happened in 1941 when the new intake of pupils arrived at the decanted Institute. By now, Admiral the Earl of Cork and Orrery had moved on and relinquished hold on the Bruce Hostel, which was again available for the girls from the country areas. Amongst the girls there was a young lass from Dunrossness (the 'ness), who must have caught my eye as I seemed to pursue her relentlessly, being spurned for years, until at last successfully entrapping her in 1953! She was Marguerite May Rosalind Black, one of five sisters from Grutness, of whom more will be written in due course.

I suppose it must have been about this time that we realised that girls were more than just people who used a different cloakroom. 'Courting' in those days consisted of walking with a few friends at a discreet distance behind the object of your intended affection and a few of her friends. This parade took place back and fore on Commercial Street after school and ended back at the lower gate of the Hostel when, if the omens and conditions were favourable, a few words might be exchanged. Walking together did not occur until the upper classes – changed days!

It must have been when we were in class III that a very serious problem arose. It had been decided that a 'beanfeast' ('proms' were still something one walked on at the seaside) would be held for the first time since the outbreak of war and that the venue would be the dance-hall of the Grand Hotel. All very well, but then the news leaked out that the organisers, classes 4, 5 and 6, had placed an embargo on the attendance of the 'sprogs' of classes 1, 2, and 3. We really could not strike or take any appropriate retaliatory action, other than to hold our own version, and that is exactly what we did. Through the good offices of the education committee (of which, coincidentally, my mother was vice-chairwoman), we were granted the use of rooms 9 and 10 in the Central and, with the big partition pulled back, there was plenty of room for all. Douglas Conochie organised the music; Bobby Groat, whose parents owned a bakery near the Malakoff, organised food supplies; and the event was a huge success. In fact, several of the teachers who had been to the 'Grand' came back to visit our festivities and appeared to enjoy the experience. None other than the headmaster, Mr Cluness, came and was cheered when he agreed to take part in the game of 'Catch the Truncher' where a wooden plate is spun and, when a name is shouted, that person must catch the plate before is stops spinning and falls.

The upper classes continued to be depleted, especially of boys, as they were called up for military service. Some had to leave school because of family circumstances, for example to take care of the family croft where all the other male members of the family were already serving in the armed forces. All this was taking place in a very different Lerwick. However, before we ended our schooldays there was the opportunity to take part in two school picnics, outings which had been suspended during the dangerous part of the war years. In 1945 there was a picnic at Sandwick, races, tug-of-war and suchlike activities. There was one slight problem, however, in that the rope for the tug-of-war was at a shop at Central in Sandwick, but help was at hand in the presence of the young lady from Grutness who had her father's car, and she, I and others set off to fetch the rope. This was undoubtedly the first time that Meg and I had been together in a car, but certainly not the last. We returned safely and the games proceeded apace.

The next picnic was in 1946, much the same format as I recall, but no need for emergency vehicles! Prior to this we had sat our 'highers' as entrance qualifications for university. Although geography was actually my favourite subject, neither lower nor higher standard were being offered as subjects at that time, history being the alternative. At that time it was necessary to have a 'group' which included both English *and* history. I was just not interested in history and that was reflected in the fact that I passed higher English at the highers in 1946 and again at the re-sits, but failed in lower history both times and unfortunately (no doubt my own blame) failed to make the necessary grade. This may be partly due to the fact that the only historical episode which I could quote with any accuracy was the American War of Independence so, no matter what question was asked, I had to respond by using that subject as the basis for an answer. This appears, to my surprise, not to have impressed the examiners! In any event, priority was being given to people returning from the armed forces whose education had been interrupted during the hostilities, so I began to look towards an inevitable period in His Majesty's Forces.

CHAPTER THREE

Wartime in Lerwick

TO set the scene, Adolf Hitler, leader of Nazi Germany, had for some time been expanding his power over various smaller countries adjoining Germany and had been warned by Britain that he must stop. Failing to heed the warnings, his troops invaded Poland on 1st September, 1939, and an ultimatum was sent to him by the British Government that he must withdraw his troops immediately.

The first signs that war was approaching may have been very evident to the older generation, but to an eleven-year-old boy there was nothing to signify that anything out of the ordinary was in the air. I do, however, remember that when, on Up-Helly-A' night, 1939, the sky was completely red overhead with a magnificent display of the merry dancers, 'they' said that this was a sign that war was coming.

The only manifestation of military might was the occasional appearance of my brother Jim, in his uniform of the 5th/7th Battalion of the Gordon Highlanders, Territorial Army. The 'Terriers' would parade for drill and training from time to time in Fort Charlotte, and this is where they were on parade at about 10am on 3rd September, 1939, having been mobilised the day before. They were waiting for orders as to when they would leave Shetland for the mainland of Scotland and possibly further afield. I can remember standing in the Fort and hearing the announcement that their departure had been delayed, and then running along to join my parents in the St Columba's Church at about 10.30am. Our family seat was right at the back of the far left rows of seats downstairs and I was able to slip into the pew without being noticed as an obvious latecomer – other than by dad! Shortly afterwards, the 'Terriers' arrived and took their seats.

This was to be a very special service as Prime Minister Neville Chamberlain was to make an announcement at 11am as to whether Hitler had responded to the ultimatum to withdraw his troops from Poland, or face war. James Halcrow, the radio technician from W. K. Conochie's, had set up a radio set and loudspeakers on the communion table in front of the pulpit and was there to see that reception was as good as possible. It should be remembered that the great majority of the older members of congregation – and the church was full – had lived through and personally experienced the horrors of the 1914-1918 war and were waiting with more dread than the enthusiasm of the younger members.

Eleven o'clock arrived and the radio gave us the following news in the faltering voice of Neville Chamberlain:

"I am speaking to you from the Cabinet Room at 10 Downing Street. This morning the British Ambassador in Berlin handed the German Government the final note stating that, unless we heard from them by 11 o'clock that they were prepared at once to withdraw their troops from Poland, a state of war would exist between us. I have to tell you that no such undertaking has been received and that consequently this country is at war with Germany."

It must have been a very sombre congregation which made its way home that morning.

A few days later the 'Terriers' left to be stationed in Aberdeenshire and the north-east of Scotland, training with other groups and undertaking guard duties at strategic points such as bridges. Soon, some were sent further afield, many being captured by the advancing German armies in France and spending the rest of the war as prisoners of war in Germany, Poland and elsewhere. Others went to Egypt as part of the 51st Highland Division to join the 8th Army – the 'Desert Rats' – and fought in the battle of El Alamein, the advance along the Mediterranean coast and the invasion of Sicily and Italy.

One remarkable coincidence took place in the town of Tripoli. My brother, Jim, had been wounded at Catania during the advance in Sicily and had been evacuated to Tripoli to have part of his arm amputated. While there, his childhood friend, Allie Gear from St Olaf Street, had been on leave and had visited Jim in hospital, then was sitting on a wall watching the vehicles moving through the town carrying troops and supplies toward the front. One truck slowed and stopped near to him and the driver came over. This turned out, believe it or not, to be my other brother, Bay, who was a bombardier in the Royal Artillery and was delivering a truck from Egypt to his unit near Tripoli. So Bay went to the hospital and saw Jim and the two brothers were able to meet under rather unusual circumstances.

Bay had also had a coincidental meeting while on the voyage from Britain to Suez. When sunbathing on the foredeck of the troopship he was astounded to hear the 'Tannoy' order Bombardier Smith A. J. to report to the bridge. In some trepidation he did so, to be greeted (maybe even with "noo dan") by the captain, one Laurence Smith from St Sunniva Street. A contemporary of Bay's, Laurence had suddenly recognised him from among the hundreds of troops on board – it is truly a small world!

However, back to Lerwick. My father had gone to Peterhead in north-east Scotland to look after the office of Andrew Smith & Schultze there, as his

With Jim and Bay, Peterhead, 1971.

partner had been called up for military service. Most of the people of military age in Shetland were now in one or other of the armed forces or merchant navy and far from home, and the local population had shrunk to about 10,000, mostly elderly, in reserved occupations, at school or unfit for service.

Soon troops began to arrive, mainly Scottish regiments, and tented camps sprang up wherever there were flat grassy areas to accommodate them. The one nearest to me was in what is now the children's playpark in King Harald Street, thereafter known as the 'Circus Camp'. I got into serious trouble on the day they arrived as, aged 11, I went to 'help' erect the tents instead of going to Sunday school as instructed. A large cargo ship with the intriguing name *Eurylochus* moored at the fish market and unloaded equipment, guns and stores. In time the tents were replaced by Nissen huts, the rounded corrugated iron structures, the remains of which can be seen today all over Shetland. Set in a hollow, the grass around the tents and huts soon became a quagmire and wooden duckboards were installed to allow the troops to progress from one hut to another without sinking to their knees in gutter. Later, tarmac pavements and parking areas were provided. Opposite the

Circus Camp.

camp, at the foot of the slope below the County Buildings, a large asbestos-clad building was erected to become the Church of Scotland canteen, where the troops could buy tea, coffee, cakes, and find rest and solace if needed.

Including RAF, Army, Navy and civilian workers, I believe that almost 20,000 military personnel were stationed in Shetland, from Unst to Fair Isle, particularly in 1940 when the threat of invasion from Norway was at its height. At that time a curfew was imposed and everyone, soldiers and civilians, had to be indoors by 11pm unless they had specific authority to be out. I can remember lying in bed at 55 King Harald Street and hearing the thunder of the soldiers 'tackety' boots as they pounded down the Town Hall Brae from dances in the Town Hall, on their way back to camp before curfew.

I shall inevitably miss out some of the installations in and around Lerwick, but I shall list the ones I remember most clearly. At the Ness of Sound and at the Green Head huge concrete bunkers were constructed to house the six-inch guns of the coastal-defence batteries, searchlights, ammunition stores and underground tunnels to protect the south and north entrances to the harbour. Frequently, firing practice would take place at night, with a target being towed by a drifter, far out to sea. This was (hopefully) illuminated by the searchlight and (again, hopefully) distinguishable from the towing vessel when the shells were dispatched. The noise was very evident, even indoors in the centre of town.

Torpedo tubes were constructed below the cemetery at the Knab, and nearby there was a boom-defence anti-submarine net which stretched across to Ham in Bressay. This was a steel mesh net supported by a floating rubber tube filled with kapok. The tube was divided into sections with hollow rubber balls and it was, for us, a great treat if storm damage caused a bit of the boom to wash ashore and we managed to 'liberate' some of the balls, as 'bouncers' were no longer available in the shops. Obviously there was a 'gate' in the middle of the boom and this was opened and shut by a drifter to allow ships in and out of the harbour. A similar operation was carried out at the Green Head. Relatively near the Green Head there was a big encampment of huts at the Point of Scatland, and another Church of Scotland canteen was provided there.

Anti-aircraft guns, either heavy 3.7-inch guns or lighter Bofors guns, were installed at places such as above Seafield House, at the Knab, at the North Ness, on the site where Cliff House (where I am writing this) was built, and on the top of the hill on Bressay opposite the harbour. There was even a mock anti-aircraft gun made up of plywood and a telegraph pole built on the point at Puller's Loch on the Sea Road, to deter possible attacks by the Luftwaffe!

In the early days, to the horror of the green-keeper, the troops who were stationed in Gilbertson Park built a gun-post with sandbags in the middle of the bowling green which was then in the park! Rumour had it that the guns were Lewis machine guns which fired .300 ammunition, but the only bullets available were .303 which were used in the soldiers' rifles. There was a 'street' with Nissen huts on either side parallel to the north boundary of the park.

Nissen huts became evident in almost every flat area in the vicinity of the town. The Royal Navy built the 'Knab Camp' outside the north-east wall of the cemetery. This unit was called 'HMS Fox' and a brass fox was placed as a wind-vane on the top of the flagpole. (The fox is now on top of the buildings at Freefield, presently occupied by 'Buildbase'.)

Another naval establishment was the camp built on the golf course near Breiwick Road for the crews of submarines who had a rest period here after missions on the coast of Norway. A third naval camp was built behind Midgarth, in Twageos Road, as accommodation for the Women's Royal Naval Service, known as the WRENS.

There were many different regiments stationed in Lerwick, and all over Shetland, and some of the more noticeable encampments were in Gilbertson Park, Hayfield, Garthspool, off Middlebie Hill (now Gilbertson Road), where the Clickimin Centre now stands, the big stores depot (CSD) which became the Shetland Marts after the war (now the site for Tesco), and many more.

A flotilla of Norwegian motor-torpedo boats was stationed in Lerwick, and to house the crews and administration staff a wooden-hutted camp was built on my father's herring curing yard, the Anglo-Scottish, at the foot of Brown's Road. In the adjoining part of Hay & Company's yard another

Nissen-hut camp was erected to house refugees escaping from German-occupied Norway.

Hayfield House was commandeered and became the headquarters for the army units stationed in Shetland.

In order to allow troops to move more speedily to threatened areas, roads were built by the military to bypass the town of Lerwick. Cunningham Way led from the waterworks, along the top of the Staney Hill, to the Gremista Burn, and McLachlan Way from near the Ladies' Drive on the old North Road down to Gremista. Just consider that these roads were built without JCBs or bulldozers. They were named after senior army officers stationed in Lerwick at the time.

Huge concrete cubes were built as tank-traps at the vehicle entrances to the town; at the top of the Sound Brae where the burn of Sound crosses the main road, and across Gremista burn. They are still there today. Concrete barriers to make vehicles stop to be searched and temporary barbed wire constructions were placed across both roads and manned by the Home Guard whenever a state of emergency was declared.

I can vividly remember one evening, I think it was a Sunday, when suddenly the streets were filled with lorries parked every hundred yards or so. The lorries were filled with armed soldiers, and my mother and many other ladies carried cups of tea to the waiting troops while they sat for hours waiting for orders. Apparently there had been a warning of imminent invasion by the Germans who were rumoured to be "at the back of Bressay". Mercifully, the threat did not materialise and after several hours the vehicles drove off again.

There were also barbed wire fences around the camps, and along the harbour-front to stop inquisitive youths from getting too near the very interesting shipping which often filled the berths. However, where there's a will, there's usually a way, and when it became known the crews of the submarines were being issued with fruit and boiled sweets, means of gaining access became urgent. Somehow or other, many of us became regular visitors to the French submarines *Minèrve* and *Rubis*, no doubt baffling the matelots with our third-year French. The skipper of the *Rubis* was, I later learned, a M.

Schlumberger, a name later associated with the oil industry in Lerwick and elsewhere. Somewhat unbelievably, on board the *Rubis* was a small dog called 'Bacchus' which took part in all the boat's wartime exploits! One slight *contretemps* might have occurred when my great friend Jeffrey Arthur, always good for a laugh, came in to Halcrow's Restaurant at the foot of Bank Lane and announced to us (entirely without foundation I must add), "Hélas! Le Général de Gaulle est mort." To our consternation, there were a few French submariners seated at a table nearby. Probably because of his disgraceful and unintelligible accent, there was no pause in their conversation and no international incident ensued!

Apart from the French, there were British, Norwegian, Polish and Dutch submarines calling regularly in Lerwick, a 'staging post' on their voyages from the main base in Dundee to and from their patrols on the Norwegian coast.

During the period in 1940 when the Allied forces were attempting to oust the Germans from the Narvik area in the north of Norway, Lerwick was a very important anchorage and repair facility for the many naval vessels which had sustained damage during action in that Arctic region. One particularly harrowing sight was that of the sloop HMS *Pelican*, which was berthed at the fish market, just opposite the foot of Harbour Street. She had been struck by bombs from two German aircraft and the bombs had actually fallen on the depth-charges on deck at the stern. Obviously there had been a massive explosion and the after-deck was curled up like an opened sardine tin. Inside the rolled up deck was the after-gun and the bodies of the gun crew. Before temporary repairs could be undertaken to allow the ship to continue to a dockyard on the British mainland, the local Malakoff shipyard workers had to cut away all of that grisly evidence.

Something which underlined the closeness of contact between people in Lerwick in those days can be illustrated by the following incident. One evening my mother and I had been visiting friends and when we came home we noticed burned-out matches on the floor of the living-room and hallway at '55'. Although my mother smoked (Balkan 'Sobranie' of course), there is no way that she would have been dropping matches all over the place. We traced the trail to the side door to our basement which led out to Cockatoo Brae and found that the door had been forced. While we were discussing what should be done, the front door bell rang, and when I answered I came face to face with Inspector 'Ike' Gray of the Lerwick Constabulary.

"Have you lost anything?" he asked, but neither my mother nor myself could really answer as we had not got round to checking. He then produced from a bag the clock which had stood all my life on our mantelpiece in the living room! It transpired that he had been investigating some other burglaries, and the suspicion had fallen on a soldier. All the various camps were being checked and 'Ike', a great family friend, had noticed the clock standing on the bedside cabinet of a certain soldier in a hut at the Point of Scatland. Having seen the clock in its 'natural habitat' on many occasions he immediately recognised it as belonging to 'Mrs Attie' and confiscated it. So the clock was duly returned to its rightful place on the mantelpiece before we knew that it was missing!

In the early days the air defences of Shetland consisted of a few Royal Air Force First World War fighters stationed at Sumburgh. These were 'Gloster Gladiators', single-seater biplanes. They were slow compared with the enemy's aircraft and, although they put up stirring displays, I don't think they could ever have caught a Heinkel, certainly not in level flight. Often being flown by young 'couldn't-care-less' students who had been members of the university air training squadrons, a Gladiator approaching Lerwick was viewed with some trepidation as they were inclined to fly down King Harald Street under the electricity wires which at that time were all above ground on poles.

The RAF Signals base in Lerwick was originally at Mitchell's Yard at the North Ness. Here they had a radio link with the Gladiators and one could listen on an ordinary radio to the operator instructing "Bamboo 1", "Bamboo 2" etc. – exciting stuff for the young folk like me. Later, a shore base for the Air-Sea Rescue high speed boats was established there. These small craft were often sent out to lie in the North Sea when raids were being carried out on Norway so that the crews of damaged aircraft had a better chance of survival should they have to 'ditch' on the way home. One of the officers on the ASR boats was Flight Lieutenant Fred Cooke, and he was billeted at '55' for a time.

Having been aroused by a messenger, he used to leave the house at all odd hours of the night and come back exhausted after hours at sea.

Having said that the approach of a Gladiator was sometimes viewed with some trepidation, I have to admit that on one occasion other aircraft were greeted with cheers and admiration. I was walking with some pals past Islesburgh House on my way home for lunch, on 22nd November, 1939, when we suddenly saw six 'planes coming over the town from the north. We cheered our air force as they swept past but we then suddenly saw the black crosses under the wings and the swastikas on the tails – they were German Heinkel IIIe aircraft from their base at Herdla near Bergen, the first signs of the enemy we had seen. They swept round and returned through the harbour on their way to attack a seaplane which was anchored in the north harbour. Crazy as it now sounds, we ran along King Harald Street and up King Haakon Street to Burgh Road so that we could see what was happening. The seaplane was on fire, and the Heinkels then flew off to the south, more-or-less over our heads, and fired their machine guns as they disappeared. One mechanic had been on board the seaplane in order to start the engines in case of a sudden gale rising so as to keep the craft safely at anchor. He managed to escape and swim ashore. Mercifully, this was still the period of the so-called 'phoney war', before the atrocities began, otherwise many of the pupils at the Central School, part of a generation of Lerwick's youth, would probably no longer have been left alive.

Later, lighthouse-keeper's wives were killed on Fair Isle and Skerries, and bairns on their way to school at Whiteness were machine-gunned but escaped uninjured. Often, if they were being chased by British fighters, the German 'planes would jettison their bombs in order to gain more speed and escape. To my knowledge this happened in the hills behind Linkster in Tingwall and, of course, beside the road on the north side of Sullom Voe. In this famous instance a very news-minded Lerwick photographer went to a butcher shop and purchased a rabbit then went by car and had his photo taken standing in the crater holding the moribund bunny! This photograph was seized on by the British press as a propaganda coup and led to the song 'Run rabbit, run', a hit for performers Flanagan and Allen.

Shetland was, of course, a very important base for all the services, being the nearest place on British soil for monitoring the movement of the powerful German battleships which would try to escape into the Atlantic Ocean to prey on convoys bringing supplies of food, fuel and war materials to our shores. Military personnel being posted here were classed as being sent 'overseas', most arriving on the troopships *Lady of Man*, *Ben-my-Chree*, *Amsterdam* or *Prague* sailing from Invergordon, or on the 'north boats' from Aberdeen. The *St Clair* had been commandeered by the Royal Navy and was now HMS *Baldur*, an armed escort ship. The *St Sunniva* became a hospital ship and was lost, carrying a complement of doctors and nurses, off the coast of Newfoundland, thought to have capsized when overloaded by ice on the superstructure. The old *St Magnus*, the *Lochnagar*, and the *Highlander* until she was sunk by the Germans, provided the link with Aberdeen, often sailing in convoy and with no regular timetable as such. In order to prevent or deter air attacks by the enemy, these ships often carried 'barrage balloons', large gas-filled balloons which were secured by a long wire to a winch on the deck of the vessel. Sometimes, when the winds were very strong, these balloons would begin to gyrate and career all over the place, finally breaking off the cable and disappearing into the skies. If the ship was moored at Victoria Pier, the errant balloons sometimes bounced off the roof of the Post Office and ended up on the top of the Staney Hill. It would then be plundered for the 'bunjee' rubber cords which provided tension under the balloons, the 'bunjee' rubber being ideal for catapults, needless to say, and hard to come by!

There is no doubt that, despite its strategic position, Shetland got off relatively lightly so far as bombing is concerned. There were, of course, attacks on Sumburgh and Sullom Voe, but given the huge amount of marine activity taking place in Lerwick harbour it seems very strange that more attention was not paid to this area by the Luftwaffe. We were aware of regular overflying of Lerwick by reconnaissance 'planes, so they were obviously aware of the activity, but I can recall only one incident when a bomb actually fell on the town. This bomb, which may well have been intended for shipping in the Freefield area, fell on a huge dump of coal which was stockpiled on a large concrete foundation at the foot of Garthspool Road. There was a Nissen hut containing administrative personnel in the vicinity, and apart from the coal being scattered in all directions, the only other damage was said to be the roof of the hut being blown off, leaving the staff sitting at their desks, completely unscathed! This was, in fact, a lucky escape as, only a few hundred yards away, there was a canteen for the troops stationed in the area in a former kippering kiln and at the time of the explosion it was full of soldiers who otherwise might have been killed or injured.

Also, because of its strategic importance, Shetland was an area with strictly controlled access, even for us as schoolchildren. We had our own identity cards and, when I went down to visit my father at Peterhead I had to have a special permit to get out of Shetland and back in again. On one occasion I lost this permit and my parents had a great deal of trouble getting it renewed, requiring the signature and authorisation of people in authority who had known me for a sufficiently long period to vouch for my allegiance to the Crown – and this at 14 or 15 years old.

Intelligence officers were stationed at different parts of Shetland, one duty being to interrogate Norwegian refugees before they were deemed to be *bona fide* and allowed into Britain. One of these was called Ronald Popperwell, who later became Professor of Scandinavian Studies at Cambridge University. He was for a time billeted with my aunts and on one occasion I called at their house when he was there and, in passing, announced that the boat was coming today. "How on earth do you know that? That is information only known to the authorities!" he exclaimed.

"Well, I just saw Attie Smith, the docker, going down to the pier wearing his dungarees, and he only works when the boat is in," I replied.

I have mentioned brother Jim being wounded, and in due course we received notification that he was on the way home, having been in hospital in England for some time. He was to arrive on the flight from Aberdeen on 21st November, 1943, and I asked permission from my class teacher to be allowed to go to Sumburgh to meet him. This was granted and I left the Central School on my way to catch the airways bus at Leask's, then operating from near the foot of Queen's Lane. On my way there a huge explosion occurred and burning debris flew all over the north end of the town. Ammunition was

Girls Training Corps, 'Salute The Soldier' week, 1944.

Boys' Brigade Band, 'Salute The Soldier' week, 1944. Me on front right.

exploding and tracer shells were flying overhead. There had been an accidental fire on board two MTBs at the pier at the Anglo-Scottish base and this had set off the explosion.

I was able to catch the bus and went to Sumburgh where I met Jim, whose first words to me were to the effect that I must never try to help him or pay any attention to the fact that he now had a wooden hand at the end of one arm – not easy I can tell you. It was absolutely amazing to see how he could, in time, tie his own shoelaces and knot his tie with one hand – just try it.

Gradually, as the Allied forces advanced through Europe, the number of military personnel in Shetland began to diminish, but the Norwegian MTBs and the Air Force remained as it was vital to keep as many German troops as possible occupied in Norway, and away from the defence of Germany, for as long as possible.

Soon it was time for Victory in Europe, the 8th May, 1945, 'VE Day' as it was called, and there were great celebrations and bonfires throughout the land. We decided to have our own bonfire and collected old wooden packing cases, any old combustible material left in the abandoned camps at the Knab and, as I recall it, waste oil from the 'picture house', all this transported on purloined shop barrows or in the cars of our more fortunate fellow conspirators. The chosen site was outside the lower gate of the Bruce Hostel, now Midgarth Crescent, no doubt with the secondary aim of impressing the Hostel residents! There were no houses nearby, still no tar on that bit of road, and it was very rough and rocky so no fear of any lasting damage to anything. The bonfire was duly lit, the flaming oil flowed down the road and it was said that the sight was very impressive – from Bressay. This was the same night that one of our contemporaries decided to try to liberate the brass 'Fox' wind-vane from the flagpole at the Knab Camp. Unfortunately (perhaps?), he could only manage to climb about half way up one of the stays so it – and he – survived.

Now began an orgy of destruction by the military authorities. Plumbing and electrical fittings in camps were smashed or, in some instances, put into trucks and driven 'over the banks' into the sea. This, in a place where everything had to be imported and where these very items would have been of immense benefit to the men returning from the war and wishing to modernise their homes. However, there was still a lot just abandoned and a certain amount of 'scranning' undoubtedly benefitted the local population. When the hospital was closed down at the Institute, a great deal of medical equipment was dumped over the Knab, in the geo on the west side at the parking area. Much of this remained on the edge and some of us retrieved such useful articles as tweezers, scalpels and clamps, vital for model-making or marquetry!

Gradually after that all the military presence disappeared but the remains of their encampments and fortifications are still visible all over Shetland to this day.

The hospital in the Anderson Educational Institute had gone, and thoughts began to turn toward the eventual return of both schools to something approaching a normal situation. But a great deal of repair and restoration had to be carried out at the Institute before the school would be ready to resume its intended role, and there was still the war against the Japanese in the Pacific to be won before 'real' peace was restored, although this war zone was so far removed from us that it sometimes seemed hardly relevant – at least to us young folk. Victory over Japan came on 15th August, 1945, and I am almost certain that we had another bonfire, this time behind the Institute.

Chapter Four

Recreation

OF course, life was not entirely occupied with school. A lot of us were keen swimmers and a dip at the Waarie Geo was always tempting if the weather was good. In fact we went in on some really stormy days and suffered frequent contact with the barnacles on the rocks as we were swept ashore when trying to land. Concrete bases for diving boards had been built there, and a 'bridge' to an outer rock, so we were well provided with all the necessary means for showing off. One 'test' which we were asked to perform by the older swimmers was to do a 'scarf-dive' and bring up a handful of sand from the bottom. Another was to swim to the 'Holley Rock' and back. Longer swims became more common as we became more proficient and I can remember a group of us, accompanied by a 'safety boat', swimming from the Waarie Geo to the Horse of the Knab, then to the Sletts Pier and back to the Waarie Geo. One big improvement which came in later years was a hut with separate changing rooms for boys and girls in the quarry above the Waarie Geo.

We also built shacks and spent a lot of time in the Knab area. Who today can identify the 'Shingly', the 'Camel's Hump', or the 'Sundial'? I shall not elaborate on our exploits in the area for fear of 'copycat' attempts which might prove costly to life or limb – something which I cannot recall ever happening in my time.

Another busy day in Lerwick was the annual regatta when swimmers competed in the 'Smaa Dock'. Usually watched by a crowd of spectators, the favourite competitions were the tub race, the greasy pole and the men's neat dive, in which I once managed a third prize. Other swimming places were at the Sandy Ayre at Twageos and the Sletts pier where diving facilities had been built, and at the Dinghy at the Ness of Sound. No warm swimming pools as yet.

Roller skating on the pavements was great fun, if not perhaps for the other pedestrian users. Two favourite places for this activity were the sale ring in the old fish market which had a smooth concrete floor, and the big concrete base at the foot of Garthspool Road, not so smooth but a much bigger area.

Sledging was also a great means of entertainment in the winter – and we seem to have had far more snow, there was far less traffic, and no salting or gritting. The pavement in Burgh Road beside View-forth, and the Town Hall Brae were my starting points, gradually progressing to Brei-wick Road, Lovers' Loan, and the 'Black Hooses', the steep slope below the Coastguard Station on the Knab. This is still a popular area but I am sure that our big wooden sledges, especially when the runners had been polished, were much faster than their present plastic counterparts. If Breiwick Road had been worked up into a really fast track and conditions were perfect it was possible, just, to set off from Knab Road near

Abby Thomason, Jim Honeyman, Jeannie Jamieson and Elsie Craigie, sledging down Breiwick Road, 1947.

43

to the Coastguard Station, turn into Breiwick Road and proceed apace down the hill, round the corner (if lucky) before the end of King Harald Street along to the foot of Sletts Road, and then either turn down over the Sletts' 'stroint' and brake before entering the sea, or alternatively turn up Sletts Road and finish at the junction with Scalloway Road. A clear run was dependent upon friends at strategic points to shout "CAAAAR" should some hindrance to our progress be seen approaching. Some brave-hearts used to go to the waterworks and come down the Sound Brae, round the original sharp corner at Baila and end up, hopefully, where the Sound Service Station now stands. This was a 'once-per-night' exercise.

Raising slides in the boys' playground of the Central School was also a regular pastime and many a bruise was suffered either by falling on the glassy surfaces or ending up, unable to stop, crashing down the steps at the bottom. This activity was usually concluded by the janitor, Mr Spalding, eventually appearing with a bucket of sand or salt, no doubt for our own good, but not met with any great acclaim, not that one would have dared to utter a word of criticism in those days.

With no TV and no youth clubs the 'youth organisations' were very popular in those days, and virtually all of the youth of the town were enrolled in one or other of those on offer. The main attractions were, for the boys, the Boys' Brigade, the Scouts, the Sea Cadets, and the Air Training Corps, and for the girls, the Girls Training Corps, the Girl Guides, the Junior Red Cross League and the Girls' Auxiliary Corps.

Together with my pals, we enrolled in the BBs in 1941 and faithfully turned up at the Central School every Friday night at 7pm to be educated and drilled into the type of youths suitable to be members of the organisation. Our captain was Jerry Andrew, just Jerry to everyone, except on Friday nights when he insisted, "It's Friday, so it's Captain da night," and our chaplain was the Rev George Smith who preached in St Olaf's Church. At that time there were 34 members in the company. One of the most popular options was to join the flute and drum band which was being established and tutored by (later Dr) T.M.Y. Manson, 'Mortimer' to all concerned. Mortimer was a patient, long suffering teacher and gradually the band numbers swelled to a

1st Lerwick Company Boys' Brigade, 1944. From left to right – back row: Geo. Manson, Andy Moncrieff, Bobby Leith, John Burgess, Andy White, Willie Arthur, Ian Fraser, Bertie Robertson, Drew Robertson, 'Skib' Johnson. 2nd row: Benny Manson, Jim Spence, Victor Burgess, Richmond Smith, Douglas Conochie, Oliver Pottinger, Douglas Smith, Arthur Isbister, Ronnie Moffat, Alan Leask. 3rd row: A. K. Robertson, Jeffrey Arthur, Jim Sinclair, Rev George Smith (Chaplain), Jerry Andrew (Captain), T. M. Y. Manson (Bandmaster), Gilbert Pottinger, William Johnson, Harry Isbister. Front row: Ian Fennel, Jim Peterson, Alec Younger, Charlie Duncan, Ray Leask, Ian Anderson, Larry Peterson, Andy Pearson.

very worthwhile 14, nine playing flutes and five drums. We played four-part harmonies, marches, hymns and even popular music on occasion. I remember that the first time Mortimer considered us fit to be heard beyond the walls of the Central we marched quietly out the South Road to where the Brevik Hospital (now Brevik House) stands and struck up with either 'Men of Harlech' or 'Onward Christian Soldiers' as we proudly marched out past the 'Matchbox', with hopefully not a soul within earshot.

Going to and from the Boys' Brigade meetings in the Central was somewhat different during the wartime from these days. There was a 'black-out' in force and everyone had to ensure that not a chink of light could be seen – this in an attempt to prevent, as far as possible, enemy aircraft being able to identify their targets. Air-raid wardens would regularly patrol the streets and if they saw a glimmer of light they would knock on the door of the house and shout, "Put out that light." The local papers have reports on people being fined up to £2 for showing lights. This, of course, meant that the streets were in total darkness and I can remember coming along King Harald Street with one hand on the wall, feeling for the part of the railings where the front gate opened. We were allowed to carry small electric torches, but the glass in front had to be covered with black paint or other material, except for a space the size of a sixpence (about 5p) and the beam, such as it was, had to be directed downwards. Vehicles also had metal louvres on the headlights, directing the light down on to the road immediately in front of the bonnet.

One very extraordinary event took place during the evening of Friday 23rd January, 1942, when we were on parade in the hall of the Central School. Suddenly there was a series of great explosions and the glass ceiling above the hall shattered. Luckily it had been covered by a thick curtain as a black-out, so the glass was stopped from falling on our heads. Captain Jerry immediately took command and shepherded us out into the air-raid shelters in the girls' playground (for some reason, only the girls' door was used on Friday nights). These shelters were large reinforced concrete structures with a 'baffle' door on each side, one facing north and one south. Everything was pitch dark of course, no street lights, and all windows in the houses and huts covered by black-out material. While we sheltered together, there was another explosion and a piece of metal rattled into the south-facing doorway. Eventually, as I recall it, an air-raid warden came along and told us that it was considered safe for us to disperse and go home. The cause of the explosions was revealed later as being large mines which had broken away from a British minefield which had been laid between the Ness of Sound and Bressay. They were driven ashore in a storm of southerly wind and swell which had been growing for days, and exploded against the rocks along the shore below the houses in Breiwick Road. A great deal of damage was caused to these properties, one roof at the Sletts being lifted right off the wallheads, and windows were broken from Breiwick Road to Commercial Street. Sadly, there was also one casualty. An air-raid warden, Walter Jamieson, who had been helping to put up shuttering over the shattered windows of one of the houses, was fatally injured by flying glass when another mine exploded. He died the following day.

During the war years there were many parades for fund-raising purposes such as 'Wings for Victory Week', 'War Weapons Week' and 'Salute the Soldier Week'. The latter took place from 6th-13th May, 1944, when the 'target' was £60,000 and the outcome was a magnificent £172,000! The band and the Company marched in the parade along with the other youth organisations and civilian and military units stationed in Shetland at the time, not in the least perturbed by the presence of the military brass and pipe bands. We also gave concert performances in Lerwick, Scalloway and Brae, and when at the camp at Mid Yell in 1944 we played in Mid Yell, Burravoe and Cullivoe, where

1st Lerwick Company Boys' Brigade Flute and Drum Band, 1944/45. From left to right – back row: Jim Spence, William Johnson, Douglas Conochie, Gibbie Pottinger, Tom Ramsay, Willie Thompson. 2nd row: Arthur Isbister, Larry Peterson. Front row: Freddy Tait, Douglas Smith, Bandmaster Manson, Captain Jerry Andrew, Drew Robertson, Ian Nisbet, Kenny Groat.

an unsuccessful attempt was made to tune the piano with a device for changing the jet on a Tilley lamp!

Gradually the band lost members, either being called up for service in the forces, finding employment elsewhere, or for personal reasons, and it is now only a happy memory. Unfortunately (perhaps) there were no tape-recorders to save for posterity our best efforts, but we seemed to be appreciated by the general public at the time – all thanks to the dedicated and occasionally unappreciated work of Mortimer and Jerry.

Jerry took command of us for the drill and physical education aspects, and I sometimes shudder to think of the antics of those of us involved in a game of 'flying angel' or 'pirates' in the Central gymnasium in which we had to use the ropes and the wallbars to avoid touching the floor and being caught by the pursuers. Amazingly, I can remember no untoward injuries other than the occasional rope-burn by landing at speed on one of the big coir mats – no soft rubbery landings in those days!

There was actually a BB Swing Band, with Oliver Pottinger on fiddle, his brother Gilbert on guitar and Jimmy Sinclair on drums, led by Corporal Douglas Conochie on piano, playing hits like 'The Sheik of Araby', 'Honeysuckle Rose' and 'Lady be Good'. Sometimes they were asked to play at venues in the country and I particularly remember two of these. The first was at a dance in the Reading Room, Baltasound, away up north in Unst. We, that is the band and camp followers, travelled up on the *Earl of Zetland* on the Friday with the intention of spending the night on the boat and returning home on the Saturday which was the normal schedule at the time. Despite a very strong wind blowing that night, the dance was a great success, but during the proceedings there was a bit of a panic as someone shouted that the ropes on the *Earl* had snapped and that she had driven ashore. Obviously nothing could be done until daylight so we were deprived of our accommodation. However, Unst hospitality was at hand, as ever, and we were all invited to spend the night with the Thomsons at Crossroads. It must have been sometime in the winter of 1945, and the services were still in evidence, as we were driven to Crossroads in a RAF truck, dodging the tea chests which were careering down the road from the pile outside the shop which formed part of the building. Next morning we rose (all from the same bed I seem to remember), and looked out the window to see that the *Earl*, having floated off on the rising tide, had sailed. Again, help was at hand, and we were transported to join the ship in Uyeasound, on the back of a lorry carrying mailbags which were covered in snow.

About the same time there was another musical outing, different venue, different band, when the famous Dixielanders played at the farewell dance for the RAF at Scousburgh Camp, at the top of the road to Clumlie at the 'ness. Once more, after the dance had finished, we were driven home in a RAF truck, this time with a very dark-skinned driver. Some length of time later when I was in the RAF and posted to London, the flat which was my billet was shared with four others including an airman called 'Flash' Gordon, who incredibly turned out to be the RAF driver who had transported us home from Scousburgh!

When the 'north boats' arrived and left from Victoria Pier in the centre of town, these arrivals and departures were a great source of entertainment for the populace. Watching cattle, cars, bags of mail, you name it, being loaded onto the boat using the old steam-driven cranes with the 'rinkle' of the chains and the smell of the steam was a never-ending delight. It was always better to keep out from under the cows when they were being slung up by a canvas strap under their bellies. The patter of the dockers was also a source of amusement. 'Mootie' Jamieson, Jeemie 'Sheeksy', 'Puffy', Whalsa' Willie, 'Lang Charlie' Edwardson and others, all great characters, and while on the subject of characters there were also Ad Jarmson, 'Pirra' Doyle, 'Slavery Mary', Hercules and Deena Boags, 'Peerie' Eddie, 'Mad' Eddie, Jackie Gear, and Harry Mundie who followed the road roller everywhere. 'Toilter' Broon, ("Hitler no got me yet!") has been recorded for posterity for the occasion when, with his ever present 'peerie dug', he was standing with a crowd of others waiting on the pier for the arrival of the boat which was delayed and said, "I wish dis boat wid come an let folk get hom ta dere beds!"

I cannot end however without the story (probably apocryphal) of Magnus and Gideon Watt who lived at the south end of King Harald Street. Soon after electricity had been installed in their home a bulb blew and

Magnie made his way to the nearest electrician's emporium to get a replacement. The assistant, wishing to know the amount of illumination required asked, "How many watts?" to which Magnie is said to have replied, "Oh, joost twa, dere joost me an Jeeds!"

There were also characters among the fishing community and one story concerns one of the lone 'Scottie' fishermen, who were often very religious people. This man was having trouble with the engine of his boat and could not remember whether the engine started on petrol and ran on paraffin or vice versa. Seeking help from the source which he trusted more than any other he got down on his knees on the deck and prayed, "Loard, Loard, a'm havin' boather wi' ma engine, an' I need ta spik wi' you yersel, an' nae the loon!"

Whatever became of today's characters? Should we look at ourselves?

Up to now there had been no sort of youth club in Lerwick, but a businessman called Stewart opened premises in a disused fish-curer's hut at (I think) Slater's yard, near Holmsgarth. Here we could play cards, table tennis and so on, but it was too far from the centre of town and was not popular in bad weather. In the meantime, Islesburgh House had been derequisitioned and was no longer required for overspill classes as the Institute would reopen after the summer break. My uncle Wilfred and his two sisters, who had occupied the house until the outbreak of war, and had been living in the meantime at 90 St Olaf Street (now Alan Owen's dental surgery), were unable to re-occupy and maintain the large property without domestic help which was not available after the war. My mother was still chairwoman of the education authority and she and others undertook negotiations with uncle Wilfred to sell the property to the authority to become the first local authority owned and run youth club in Shetland. This substantial, well-built property was ideally situated in the centre of town, with large rooms for the various clubs which soon became established with Mr Victor Spalding as warden. Among the first to thrive were the '500' club and the radio club, with the camera club hard on their heels. I still have my original membership card, No. 49, having paid my annual subscription of 2/6 on the 23rd September, 1946.

Surely one of the great success stories in Lerwick, the Islesburgh Youth Club moved into the former Central School and became the Community Centre, while Islesburgh House was transformed into the very successful Youth Hostel. Having known the building when it was a family home, I was very pleased and impressed with the workmanship which had been devoted to the restoration and conversion of the property.

I have not mentioned (apart from my non-attendance because of assisting the military to become established in the Circus Camp) attendance at church or Sunday school, which was another inescapable outing as my parents were regular churchgoers at St Columba's where dad was an elder. One other occasion where I and others were apparently at fault was when, on our way along the South Hillhead, we had to take shelter behind a wall because a German 'plane suddenly began machine-gunning the cable-ship *Ariel* which was anchored in the harbour. This made us arrive at the kirk a bit late whereby we incurred the wrath of the superintendent, Lowrie Cogle, who insisted that, if we had been on time, we would have been in no danger.

Different ministers have different ideas as to how to interest their captive audience. I can remember the change in attendance and enthusiasm at the bible class when the Rev W.C.B. Smith took charge. He had been a chaplain in the 51st Highland Division at the fighting in North Africa and his sermons were often based on his own experiences which were much more enthralling to my age-group than the sometimes difficult to understand (or sometimes, believe) texts which previously were more the norm. I can remember one occasion when we of the senior bible class were helping to redecorate the vestry, and Rev Courtland Smith was on top of a step ladder painting while singing a (very slightly risqué) military ditty. Suddenly the outer door opened and in came one of the elders, Donny Sutherland, plumber of this parish. He looked, listened and withdrew immediately, this being neither the posture nor pronouncements expected of the minister of the 'Big Kirk', especially *in* the Big Kirk!

'Cotie' Smith was also a boxing 'blue' from his university and it was rumoured that he had put this to good use on one occasion to indicate his displeasure with the behaviour of one of his parishioners.

CHAPTER FIVE

Serving King and Country

IN the summer of 1946 a letter summoned me to attend the YMCA (now the TA Hall) in Fort Charlotte where I would be examined by a doctor and assessed for fitness for military service. The doctor was Roy MacKenzie, our family doctor, but he still went thoroughly over me, introduced me to my first FFI (into which I will not go further!) and announced that I had flat feet. This, apart from my defective eyesight, immediately and obviously put paid to me becoming an ace fighter pilot, so I slunk away to await the call-up papers to arrive.

Eventually instructed to appear at RAF Padgate near Warrington, on 6th December, 1946, I duly arrived with half a train-load of others at the nearest railway station about 0900 to be loaded into RAF lorries and driven to the camp to raucous shouts of, "Get your knees brown!" from others who had been in the 'mob' for at least a week! Breakfast of bacon, sausage, egg and beans, was served to the hungry masses but, deeply imprinted in my memory, is the fact that it had been prepared for the first shift at 0600, so was not as palatable as we might have wished, congealed on cold plates, at 1000. We were duly enlisted and registered as being in Group 78, the last intake before national service began in January, 1947. This meant that we were conscripted for 'D of PE' – Duration of Present Emergency – which, in effect, meant without limit of time, whereas national service was for a limited time of 18 months, later two years. My number, never to be forgotten, was 2336407, and my last three now form part of my email address. In preparation for this chapter I have just been looking at my 'Service and Release Book' and discover for the first time that, to my surprise and amusement, my date of birth is given as, and is copied in other documents as, 31.3.48. This means that I was enlisted two years before I was born!

Service in the forces was an education in life which I have never forgotten or regretted. Being from such a remote and insular place as Shetland I had never met the type of people who were going to be my daily comrades-in-arms for the foreseeable future. Among them were an illiterate miner from Durham, a French-speaking chef, and Ricky, a small, wiry and ruthless ex-barber from the Gorbals in Glasgow, who invariably used to return late from leave, having been a guest in Barlinnie or some other such establishment. He actually used to cut our hair using a cut-throat razor! My best pal turned out to be 2336419 Dave Sharples from Stockport who, despite having lost two and a half fingers on his right hand in a steel rolling-mill where he was an apprentice, was still deemed fit to pull a trigger.

Having been presented with our uniforms, we were soon off to our 'squarebashing' camp at West Kirkby, on the Wirral near Liverpool. This was January 1947, and I suspect that some folk will remember that this was the winter with the great snowfall, accompanied by a coal strike whereby only specific trains carrying coal to vital establishments were allowed to move across the network. As the effects of the strike spread, more and more of the camp at West Kirkby was closed down and the airmen sent on leave. By some mischance, 4 Wing, in which we were based, was kept on site to ensure that the heating systems for the sick bay, admin offices and, of course, officers' quarters, were kept in operation. Heating in the huts was provided by a 'Bogey' stove in the middle of the floor, and we had to use all our ingenuity to ensure that we at least had enough fuel for a fire in the evening. Sometimes we were able to purloin some coke from one of the dumps, and sometimes we had to resort to tearing up floorboards in the unlocked porch of one of the now unoccupied huts. Our drill instructor, Corporal Whitehouse (I kid you not, and not always pronounced correctly!), was aware that something was going on but he also was living in the same hut so benefitted from the heat as well and never made any comment.

My friendship with Dave Sharples meant that I was sometimes invited home with him to Stockport when we had a '48' (48-hour pass). We also used to go to Liverpool when we had time off and I used to enjoy riding on the overhead railway past the docks where great liners and many merchant ships were still to be seen. One day, when walking through a street in Liverpool where some bomb damage had still not been repaired, I saw two policemen who were examining a boarded up door. In passing I distinctly heard one of them say, "This corrygated iron is loose." Now 'corrygated' is the Shetland pronunciation so I went back and enquired as to his roots. To my amazement this turned out to be Gibby Andrew, brother of Jerry, my erstwhile captain in the Boys' Brigade. Sadly, while writing this chapter, I learned of Gibby's death.

Eventually, toward the end of March, we had our passing-out parade and we were sent home on leave. I was given half a meat pie as rations for the journey and a railway warrant to Shetland which I had to negotiate with the North of Scotland Shipping folk in Aberdeen before I was allowed to get on the boat. In company with many Shetlanders, if we had to spend a night in Aberdeen a bed was always available at the Seamen's Home, where the genial and helpful host was Jim Groat from Lerwick.

This was the year when virtually all the roads in Shetland were blocked by the great snowfall and supplies were being delivered around the coast by the *Earl of Zetland* and other boats. I decided to try to have a few days extra leave and sent a telegram to the authorities that the roads to Walls were blocked, which was quite true although, living in Lerwick, I could see the steamer coming and going. I received instructions to 'proceed when conditions improved' – which I duly did – and got away with it!

Because of the possibility that the roads could be blocked for a prolonged period, the pupils in Class VI from the country areas who were about to sit their 'highers' were not allowed to go home, so were 'marooned' in Lerwick. This worked to my advantage as I was able to renew my hitherto somewhat distant acquaintanceship with Meg, particularly enjoying the close contact achievable (albeit usually with several others) on the sledge in Breiwick Road. However, eventually and reluctantly, I had to accept the fact that the boat was available and set off south once more.

My first posting was to the Rail Transport Office (RTO) at King's Cross in London where many of those passing through were heading home on 'demob leave'. One of these turned out to be Angus Laurenson from St Olaf Street, who later became a teacher at the Institute. He got a surprise when I asked him to go across to '55' and tell my mother that we had met. My billet at that time was in a block of flats at Viceroy Court, opposite Regents Park Zoo. It was a very pleasant experience, and I was able to visit my aunt and uncle at Glendoone during my time off.

However, this was too good to last and the powers that be decided that the time had come for training to take up a trade in the 'mob'. Having already realised that my dream of being an ace fighter pilot was no longer achievable, and in any event the hostilities had ended, I discovered that I had been chosen to be employed in the next most important position – a 'storebasher' in the equipment section (what can operate without spares?) – and was summoned to report to RAF No. 2 School of Admin Trades at Credenhill, Hereford (now the headquarters of the SAS).

Herefordshire is a beautiful county and the weather was perfect, but my enduring memory of Credenhill is my first – and last – encounter with 'scrumpy', the vicious concoction produced from apples which has a kick like an ostrich, mainly felt in the head! I was at Credenhill from July until September 1947, then went to be on permanent staff at RAF Bridgnorth in Shropshire. This was another 'squarebashing' camp. Being on permanent staff meant that we were in a separate hut from the recruits and, as the hut was also occupied by cooks and drivers, we had the benefits of food at all hours of the day and night and the chance of lifts into the nearby town. Bridgnorth is a town built on two levels with a steep funicular railway linking the two, so a lift made life much easier when available. One day I was looking out of the window in the stores office when a group of recruits was passing 'at the double'. I did a 'double-take' as I was sure that I actually recognised the legs and running action of one of the group. On checking at the appropriate hut I found my school chum, Jeffrey Arthur, from 58 Breiwick Road – another 'small world' encounter – and there was also a Johnson boy from Voe in the same group. We were able to have a few evenings together and exchange 'home news' which was a great change from the usual barrack-room chatter.

Me, 'Whitey' and Jeffrey Arthur, RAF Bridgnorth, 1947.

While at Bridgnorth there came the chance to apply for a posting nearer home, so I applied, hoping perhaps even to get to the Observatory in Lerwick where there were still a few RAF stationed at the Met. station. However, the outcome was that I next did a spell of duty at RAF Kinloss in Morayshire – at least it was a bit nearer home and gave me a chance to meet up again with Douglas Conochie, who was then at Aberdeen University.

Kinloss was then a base for Lancaster bombers, parked all round the airfield, mostly waiting to be scrapped, but some were still undertaking training flights over the North Sea. My duty there was as 'petrol king' mainly involved with filling 'bowsers' with the different types of aviation fuel required by different aircraft. There were also seemingly endless guard duties to preserve the security of the parked aircraft and the sanctity of the enormous boundary fence. However, I had hardly settled in at Kinloss when I received word that I had been posted overseas and went home on 10 days 'embarkation leave'.

I was to report to No. 5 PDC (Personnel Despatch Centre) at Burtonwood, the massive former American air base near Warrington, so my earlier journey to Padgate was about to be virtually repeated. No information was forthcoming as to our destination, but an uncomfortable day spent in medical checks and injections – none of your modern sharp needles here, a thing like a knitting needle stuck into the arm and then different syringes attached and squirted as we passed along a row of grinning medics. Then we were issued with our 'KD' (khaki drill) jackets, shorts and so on, so it appeared that we were going somewhere warm. (Not always the case, as it is said that, during the war, some airmen arrived at Sullom with KD gear whereas their intended destination was actually Sollum in North Africa!)

We left by train for Southampton and prepared to board the P & O ship *Otranto* which, at 22,000 tons, was the largest liner I had yet seen, but she was in fact dwarfed by the old *Queen Mary* which we passed on our way out Southampton Water. We were allocated bed spaces and a table in the mess area and settled in as best we could. I have omitted to say that among the hundreds of others on board ship was my old mate Dave Sharples, so we chummed up again. However, like most of the others, he had never been on board any form of floating vessel in his life! The voyage across the Bay of Biscay was very rough and most of those at my mess table were unable to eat until we arrived in calmer waters nearing Gibraltar. They could not stay in bed, however, as everyone had to be clear of the sleeping accommodation and on deck by 1000, so the decks were covered with miserable-looking people in various recumbent positions for the first couple of days. I and a chap from the Western Isles managed to survive the experience, but had to minister to our less-well comrades as best we could.

We stopped at Gibraltar for a few hours and then sailed on to Valetta in Malta. The weather had improved, but this was still the end of January so not all that warm at sea. At Valetta we were in the company of a large American warship with a military band playing on the afterdeck. Off again after a short stop and on to the Piraeus, the port for Athens in Greece. Very noticeable here was the poverty among the boatmen. The *Otranto* was anchored off in the harbour and barges and small boats were being used to unload cargo. The people on these boats were dressed in rags and were begging us to throw them anything we had to spare – soap seemed to be a particular favourite as

I remember. The next stop on our Mediterranean cruise was Salonika where conditions were similar to those at Piraeus.

The final part of our voyage was from Salonika to Port Said in Egypt, and then we knew that this was our intended destination. Anyone who has arrived at Port Said in a troopship will remember the scene with dozens of 'bum boats' at the sides of the ship, lines thrown on board by the so-called worthy oriental gentle-folks and baskets of goods supposedly to be hauled on board when payment was thrown down. What horrified us, the 'green' new arrivals, were the actions of the hardened crew of the *Otranto* who had no compunction in using the fire hoses to wash off any unauthorised person trying to climb onboard, and if they succeeded, in throwing them back into the Suez Canal. It took a surprisingly short time for us to be just as casual about the thieving natives who were adept at snatching watches off one's wrist or picking pockets while being distracted by another selling 'eggs-a-bread' or inviting one to share the available charms of his sister.

On the quayside we were lined up and a flight sergeant with pacing stick walked along the front row, stopped two places from me and told the group he had just passed to turn right and march off with their kit. We later discovered that they had been sent to Palestine where several lost their lives in the insurrection which was taking place there at the time. The rest of us were put on a train and, on the way south, we had our first glimpse of the Canal Zone which was to be our home area for the foreseeable future. The railway ran more-or-less parallel to the Suez Canal and it was fascinating to see great liners apparently steaming through a sea of sand, with palm trees and camels adding character to the scenery.

Our final destination was 107 Maintenance Unit which lay about half way down the west side of the Great Bitter Lake at a place called Kasfareet. The name may be familiar to those of a choral nature who have participated in the ditty whereby the singer had passed that area with nothing to eat, having thrown all his rations away to the displeasure of the captain of the good ship 'Somersetshire'.

Anyway, there we were at the end of the road and having to gear up to a life in a different country and different climate. This was now the beginning

With Dave Sharples, 107 M.U., Kasfareet, Egypt, 1948.

of February so it was still cold enough for us to be wearing our RAF 'blues', the KD being worn after the 31st March. The repatriation of German prisoners of war had not yet been completed and there was a large area within the outer perimeter fence which was designated as a secure area for the POWs. 'Secure' was not really an appropriate word as the wall round their encampment was made of mud and only about four inches high, but there was only one point at which they could come out of and go into their compound. There was also a tower with an armed guard and searchlight overlooking their enclosure and anyone venturing over the 'wall' was liable to be shot.

There were large quantities of valuable supplies, arms and ammunition stored in the camp and, apart from the high barbed wire perimeter fence, there were guard towers with powerful searchlights every hundred yards or so with orders to shoot on sight if intruders were spotted. Several German prisoners had escaped from different camps and were intent on stealing arms and ammunition to help the insurgents fighting in Palestine, and the Egyptian population in the nearby villages was not entirely averse to owning bits of kit or spares from vehicles or aircraft should they appear available! The Germans within the camp, however, appeared to be content with their lot and were patiently awaiting repatriation to their devastated homeland. Inside their secure area they had built a real German beer-garden using spare wood and scrap materials. 'Stella' Egyptian beer and gramophone records completed the atmosphere in this desolate sandy place, and the entertainment was even enjoyed by the poor chap on guard duty up the tower.

My duties here were in the stores section which was manned by a corporal; myself; Mr Tanti, a Maltese civilian; Fritz, a German prisoner of war; and Chico, a small Egyptian boy who fetched and carried, made tea, etc. Fritz had been a leading stores technician in the Luftwaffe and knew more about aircraft stores and organisation than any of us – certainly more then me! He knew where every nut, bolt rivet and tool was kept – I'm almost certain under the Luftwaffe stores system – so, until he was repatriated, the rest of us had a very easy life.

The Germans on the camp really had a relatively easy life as well, being set to work in their pre-war and wartime trades where possible. For example, the food in all the messes on camp was prepared by German chefs from high class hotels, and the drop in standards when they left was somewhat noticeable! Similarly, the camp had a sailing-club on the Great Bitter Lake and boat-builders from the Hamburg yacht club spent their time building yachts from discarded mahogany packing cases – it should be noted that the Commanding Officer at Kasfareet was a keen sailor.

Because of the soaring temperatures, work usually stopped before the height of the day and I, along with many others, made for the yacht club and relaxed in, or at least near, the water. Before one was allowed to skipper a boat at the club, one had to pass the exam set by the British Royal Yachting Association. Having achieved this, together with another sailing enthusiast, Irishman Paddy Byrne from Ballymena, I bought a 'Snipe' dinghy by instalments from a member who was going home and spent as many hours as possible sailing either for relaxation or in the various regattas.

A favourite jaunt was across to the opposite side of the Great Bitter Lake where there was a concealed lagoon which, needless to say, was named the

'Blue Lagoon'. Mainly for this reason I was never really tempted to visit the Street of a Thousand Aerosols in Cairo or the other historic sites in Egypt. At Whitsun, 1948, there was a regatta at Ismalia on the Lesser Bitter Lake (Lake Timsah) and our boats were being towed up the Suez Canal by a safety boat when a large liner was seen coming in the opposite direction. Because of the displacement of the vessel, the level of water in the canal rose sharply as it passed, so we had to lie at the side until it had passed. I was in the last boat in the string and, as we set off again I saw a bit of wood in the water. Being a true Shetlander, I leaned over and salvaged it. You can imagine my surprise when I read the advert on it – 'L Williamson, Fishcurer, Scalloway'. The side from a kipper box thrown overboard from some passing ship! This was the only time I can remember ever being really homesick.

There were other reminders of home not far away, however. When I was standing in a queue waiting to collect the billet laundry, a voice suddenly said, "Isn't it Duggie Smith?" This was none other than Bertie Laurenson from Uradale, near Scalloway, whom I had last seen as a classmate in Class 5 at the Institute the previous year. He could tell me that Jim Sinclair, another former classmate, from Seafield Court at the south end of Commercial Street, and Drewie Nicolson from King Harald Street were also stationed nearby – it is undoubtedly a small world.

The village of Kasfareet consisted of a few mud huts on the side of the Sweet Water Canal – a misnomer if there ever was one. Its filthy water was used for every purpose imaginable (and I do mean *every*!) and how the population survived must have been a miracle of some kind. Certainly there appeared to be no aid of any kind and the contrast between the lifestyles of the villagers and that of the then rulers, King Farouk and Queen Farida, was indescribable. (Certain barrack-room ditties also featured the King and his expectant wife.) Watching the ever-changing procession of big liners with the black box containing a searchlight hanging on the bow, waiting in the Great Bitter Lake for clear passage north to the Mediterranean or south to the Red Sea, was a daily change of scenery from the endless expanse of sand and grit which stretched around us. Again, for me, this was another lesson in education for life, something I would never otherwise have seen at such close quarters.

The phrases 'roll on the boat' and 'boat happy' began to be heard more and more as the time drew closer to the day when those of us ready for demobilisation would once again be in Port Said, but this time to board the troopship for the voyage home. In my case this was on the 13th February, 1949, almost exactly a year since I had arrived. Still in the company of Dave Sharples, I boarded the *Empire Prince* and we set off on the 10-day voyage to Southampton. This was no calm blue Mediterranean but a grey windswept and rough bit of water, and I think that everyone was pleased to have a couple of hours of calm water in the harbour at Gibraltar before we faced the Bay of Biscay once more. However, the last part of the voyage was relatively calm and we duly arrived at Southampton. On the last stage of the trip there was an announcement that we could take only 100 cigarettes into the country and threatening dire punishments for anyone who tried to smuggle anything ashore. On the voyage from Port Said we had been issued with tins of 50 cigarettes almost every second day, so there was a frantic throwing overboard of hundreds of tins full of fags as we sailed up Southampton water – someone on the Isle of Wight must have profited I am sure as these were hermetically sealed tins.

Once ashore and cleared by customs – and they were thorough – we boarded trains and set off for our various destinations. The RAF contingent was bound for Preston Station and then Warton, near Blackpool (now the airfield where the Eurofighter is built and tested). For some reason or other my papers, and those of some others, had been mislaid at Southampton so, while the majority went to bed, we had to remain in the admin department while a despatch rider was sent from Southampton with the missing documents. Having been on our feet for some hours before we actually came ashore, this was about the most exhausting experience I had during all my service!

However, all was well in the end, and the following morning, the 25th February, 1949, I was presented with my grey pinstripe demob suit, paddy hat, etc., and delivered by truck to Preston Station to catch the train to Aberdeen as a civilian. This is where I said farewell to Dave Sharples who went south to Stockport, while I headed north. However, we kept in touch, right up until his death in 2007. I spent a few days with dad at Peterhead and then caught the boat home. This was another experience as we took 23 hours to reach Lerwick, only arriving about 1500, to be met at the gangway by Allie Arcus, the then manager of Lerwick Thistle who was keen to sign anyone he knew before their feet touched the pier! Then it was home to a greatly changed lifestyle from what I had been experiencing, and occasionally enduring, for the past twenty-seven months.

A few odd (in every sense of the word) words of Arabic still occasionally come to mind, and chance meetings with the Rev Jim Blair on Commercial Street invariably produce at least "Saida Effendi!" Having been in action in Egypt with the 8th Army I suspect that he also has a reasonable command of the essential additional vocabulary prevalent in the region.

CHAPTER SIX

Civvy Street

MY mother had been virtually on her own since I left in December 1946, as, while I was serving 'King and Country', dad and Jim had been following the herring for much of each year. It was now something of a change for her to have me home and under her feet again. It was also very strange for me to be in Lerwick to find that almost all my erstwhile friends were now away at university or college. I found it difficult to settle down, and must have been a bit of a trial to mum.

As I said earlier, my mother was a small, deceptively frail looking person but was strong-willed, wiry and possessed of endless energy. One of the first women graduates from Aberdeen University, she seemed to have almost unlimited knowledge which she could express in a most forceful way, which served her well when, in later years, she became chairwoman of the Zetland Education Authority. She was also an accomplished musician, playing the piano, singing and producing the Gilbert and Sullivan operas which were performed in Lerwick before and after the First World War. She was also called upon to be part of the group which was formed to entertain the troops stationed in Shetland during World War Two, and travelled from Sumburgh to Sullom Voe with a group performing Gilbert and Sullivan selections on several occasions.

The group had, really since I was born, practised in the drawing room on the first floor of 55 King Harald Street, where our piano was situated. This room was, coincidentally, next to my bedroom so I grew up, and fell asleep night after night, to the music of 'Three Little Maids from School', 'A Wandering Minstrel I' or 'A Policeman's Lot is Not a Happy One'! This must

My mother at the piano in 55 King Harald Street.

have instilled into me the love that I have for music, whether taking part or just listening.

We were also fortunate in having a good piano as, during the war years, there were many professional musicians stationed in Shetland in the forces and they would come to practise at various private houses, including our house and that of my aunts, Daisy and Flora, at 89 King Harald Street. The ones I can best remember were David Wolfstahl and Edward Rubach, a brilliant duo with violin and piano, who performed regularly on the radio after the war. Dr Melville Cook, a lowly bombardier in the Royal Artillery stationed at the Castle Camp, where Sandveien now stands, was a brilliant musician and had been organist at Hereford Cathedral. After the war he took up the same post at Montreal Cathedral. It was a joy and a unique experience to sit beside the piano while these gifted people were exhibiting their skills. I can also remember a jazz group who were then stationed at RAF Sullom Voe (I think it was Harry Gold's 'Pieces of Eight'), practising before playing somewhere in Lerwick. My Aunt Anna tried for a while to teach me to play the piano but, like so many others, I preferred football and would not practise – to my great shame and disappointment now.

Famous performers of the day also came to Shetland to perform to the troops and, although it was usually impossible to get inside the Garrison Theatre, we could stand outside and hear the performances through the ventilators. Nat Gonella, George Formby and Gracie Fields were perhaps the

The Campbell sisters: Flora, Jennie, Mary and Daisy, at Scousburgh.

most well known. Gracie Fields actually had a 'spill-over' audience in the Town Hall where the programme was broadcast live and civilians including myself were able to enjoy her unique talents. I can remember that she sang 'Coming Home on a Wing and a Prayer' for the first time when in Lerwick.

Not able to participate I was, however, able to enjoy the performances of others like the Dixielanders with Douglas Conochie, and later my cousin Alex Campbell, on piano, Jim Irvine on drums, Freddy Tait on clarinet, Jim 'Dinky' Spence on trumpet and, of course, Peerie Willie Johnson on guitar and double bass. Many an interesting evening was spent at dances in the Rechabite Hall in Mounthooly Street, where the interval music was provided by the ever-present Mrs Mustard on piano. Sometimes we even ventured farther afield. I can remember going to a summertime dance in the Sand Hall, an ex-army wooden hut. We were driven by James 'Pinkie' Wiseman at breakneck speed in an ex-army shooting brake, arriving about 10.30 to find the hall virtually empty. "De're no feenished wi' de hay yet," was the explanation, but eventually things got under way and we arrived home sometime after sunrise, tired but happy.

Occasionally there were performances by local concert parties in premises such as the Twageos Hall – a Nissen hut between South Ness House and the road. Who could ever forget Tammy Walterson playing solos with a fiddle bow on a saw!

It was said that no Shetland concert was ever a success without a cowboy song and a joke about a shanty (not the sea variety)!

I had arrived home in February, just about six weeks before my 21st birthday at the end of March. In those days it was the 21st rather than the 18th which was celebrated and my parents decided to give me a 'Welcome-Home-plus-21st-Birthday' party in the Grand Hotel. This was an excellent way of renewing contact with all my friends, many of whom I had really not seen for more than two years including, of course, Meg, to whom I had sent the odd letter and photo during my enforced absence! As this also fortuitously coincided with end-of-term holidays at universities and colleges I was able to invite many who would otherwise have had to be omitted. I seem to remember that it was considered a great success, and it certainly was a great 'hamefarin' for me.

Having been 'cornered' by Allie Arcus I duly signed and played for Lerwick Thistle, and subsequently for 'Hibs' under the management of Archie Hutchison.

I then went down to Peterhead and spent some time with dad and Jim, occasionally travelling in to and out from Aberdeen on the old utility buses with ribbed wooden seats which did nothing for the posterior on the hour-and-a-half-long journey! While in Aberdeen I bought a racing bike with a fancy 'De Railleur' gear-change system. This later stood me in very good stead over many years and many miles on the road between Lerwick and Grutness.

About this time a group of us were regularly spending weekends at the very hospitable home of the Black family at Brake, Quendale. Together with Jimmy Rendall, Abby Thomason and others, we spent a lot of time kicking around a football on the Quendale links and someone, probably John 'Chinky' Irvine, had the idea of forming a football team. With the cooperation of Leslie

Eunson, who built up another team (which included the local minister, Rev Ferguson) in Bigton, we began to have regular games on Saturday evenings. One week we played on Quendale links and the next on a field inside the gate of Bigton Farm. One slight problem was the number of rabbit holes at Quendale and, if players caught their foot in a hole and fell, they were often heard uttering not very Christian epithets then, remembering that the Rev Ferguson was only a couple of feet away, had to seek immediate absolution! Next to form a team was 'Queen of the South' at Sumburgh, with the pitch on the airfield when there were no aircraft using it! I then joined Queen of the South which, of course, allowed me to 'flit' to the other hospitable Black household at Grutness. In due course, Sandwick joined in and then Cunningsburgh and the Southern Football League was born. This led to the

Queen of the South, 1954. Back row: D. C. Smith, R. Peterson, L. Leslie. Middle row: J. Harper, J. Aitken, J. Brown, A. Peterson, L. Aitken. Front row: A. Flaws, D. Black, D. Young.

formation of Ness United, under the management of George Gocke, and participation in the Shetland Football Association competitions. I am sure many will still remember the *après football* dances in the Virkie Gym, the former RAF gymnasium and cinema. Meg's father had a 15-cwt ex-RAF pick-up which was known as the 'Buggy' and it formed an excellent grandstand for his wife Mary and other supporters on the touchline at home matches!

This is when my trusty bike came into its own and I cycled from Lerwick to Grutness at weekends whenever possible and often got a lift half-way back to Sandwick from Meg in her dad's car. This indicates, I think, that my intentions were getting serious.

I decided to have one last attempt at getting the elusive lower history (which still had to be sat along with higher English) so did some 'crash' revision and attended at the Cowdray Hall, Aberdeen University, in August 1949. Yet again, the inevitable happened; I passed higher English for the third time but failed lower history. This was enough for me, so it was back home to look for a job which did not require a detailed knowledge of history.

CHAPTER SEVEN

'Da Coonty'

IN the *Shetland News* I saw an advert for an apprentice sanitary inspector for Zetland County Council. Not having a clue what that meant or entailed, my mother decided that I should, whatever the outcome, make enquiries and I therefore made an application and was granted an interview.

To first set the scene, which was somewhat different from today, one room in Brentham Place contained the medical officer of health, Dr Black, and his staff, which consisted of his secretary, Cathy Tulloch. There were also some district nurses in Lerwick and the country areas. Dr Black and his family occupied the top flat as their dwelling house. In another room was the county sanitary department, which comprised the county sanitary inspector, W.L. Hastings, and his staff, which included his secretary, Joey Halcrow, and an apprentice. The remainder of that floor was occupied by the education department under the director, John H. Spence, and his staff. (I think that adding up the staff numbers these days might produce a somewhat inflated figure.)

The apprentice sanitary inspector had resigned when he discovered that he was expected to obtain some qualifications which would require him to study at a college outwith Shetland. This he was not prepared to do.

I therefore presented myself at Brentham Place and met for the first time, my future boss, William L. Hastings. I never addressed him as anything but 'Mr Hastings' and propose to use that method in this chapter.

Born in the village of Airth, near Falkirk, Mr Hastings had, so far as I could learn from him during the years we spent together, a hard upbringing in this area renowned at that time for mining and heavy engineering. Having studied and qualified as a sanitary inspector, he first worked in his home area and then, when the opportunity arose during the war years, he applied for and was appointed to the post of county sanitary inspector for Zetland County Council. With no staff other than a secretary, and working under the stringent restrictions of wartime, it must have been very difficult for anyone to come into this remote and scattered community and supervise compliance with the (at that time) 51 Acts, Orders, and Regulations under his control. I have a list of these statutory instruments and many were still being enforced during the years I worked in, and latterly headed, the department. The Public Health (Scotland) Act, 1897, was the 'bible' which more or less covered every known and possible relevant situation! Also at that time, and until local government reorganisation in 1974, the appointment of county sanitary inspector was a statutory appointment and had to be approved by the Secretary of State for Scotland, as also had the removal of such person from office.

So, here I was, ready to be interviewed. Being 21, and having had the experience of life in the forces, I suppose I was a bit more mature than someone applying at age 17 or 18. I really cannot remember if there was anyone other than Mr Hastings who carried out the interview but I am inclined to think not. I suppose in a similar situation today there would be at least one councillor, a representative from the personnel and perhaps finance departments, and maybe even somebody to give me counselling if I failed to make the grade! Be that as it may, I passed the interview and was offered the job in a letter dated 27th September, 1949, to commence work on a probationary footing on Monday, 3rd October. One interesting paragraph from my 'Conditions of Apprenticeship' reads as follows: 'Annually during the months October to March, the apprentice will attend a four years' course of training at a recognised Training College in preparation for the examination for the Sanitary Inspector's Certificate of the Royal Sanitary Association of Scotland, and during those periods he shall receive no salary from the Council.' I can understand now why the earlier incumbent decided to change his job! However, the matter having been discussed with my parents, they decided to support me during the four winters which I would have to spend out of Shetland and without support from my employer. I therefore accepted the offer. This was confirmed at a meeting of the health executive sub-committee on 11th October, and I began my life-time of service with the council on the salary of £80 per annum (that meant £40 for the six months during which I was to be paid)!

One problem was that the term at the Heriot-Watt College in Edinburgh, which I had decided to attend, started in mid-September, so I was too late to enrol for the session 1949-50. It was therefore decided that I would gain practical experience in Shetland until the beginning of the term in September 1950. Although they were very different departments, Dr Black, as medical officer of health, was nominally in charge of the sanitary department as well. This, I may add, was never accepted by sanitary inspectors, and in some instances the working relationships were far from cordial. This was never the case in Shetland, certainly so far as I was concerned, one MoH saying to me when he took up office, "You do your job and I'll do mine, but get it wrong and I'll have you!" That suited me down to the ground and we had an excellent working relationship for the many years he remained in Shetland.

My first work experience was actually on my first day in the office, accompanying Dr Black to Sandwick to act as a witness when he was carrying out a statutory inspection. He was a very kind and understanding family man, and patiently explained to me the legal niceties of the task in which we were involved.

The main change in housing conditions in Shetland, which really govern the standard of living, began to become apparent in the immediate post-war years. Young men and women who had been serving in the forces and had become used to the presence of piped supplies of hot and cold water, showers or baths and indoor toilets, were now coming home to old-fashioned cottages with water carried from wells, hot water heated on the stove and baths in a zinc bath on the kitchen floor. Some had 'Elsan' chemical closets, some had pails in the byre and some had none whatsoever.

I can give one example of the latter where I was personally involved. When I had become sufficiently trusted to be sent out on my own, I had been sent to a remote part of the North Mainland where it was on record that a certain property had no sanitary facilities. It was my task to persuade the elderly male occupant that it would be in his own interests to install at least an 'Elsan', but my persuasive powers were getting nowhere! "I have no need for dat," he said, "I just geen ti da hill dik (dyke)."

"But," I said, "what if it is raining or snowing?"

"Dan I joost tak a sheet o' corrygated iron ower mi head," was the response.

I decided that, in the light of this impasse, I was not going to get anywhere so returned to the office to report to higher authority.

There was piped water and an antiquated drainage system in Lerwick and Scalloway but virtually nowhere else unless it was to an individual private house. Of course, the drainage merely consisted of fireclay pipes which followed the most convenient contour leading as straight as possible into the sea. There was no treatment whatsoever and, in Lerwick for example, there was raw sewage being discharged more-or-less all along the foreshore. Add to this input from the hundreds of men in the crews of the fishing boats in the harbour and the thousands of fishworkers on the curing stations during the summer season, and it was a blessing indeed that the harbour had two entrances to allow the tides to flush out the pollution – was 'pollution' ever mentioned or considered? We happily swam in the smaa dock!

The vast majority of houses in the rural areas were, frankly, 'unfit for habitation' in terms of the relevant acts. The young folk then faced the mammoth task of modernising their family homes, not always with the willing support of their parents who thought that "what had done them for years would just do fine for a while longer". Then there was a chronic shortage of building materials, vast quantities being required to rebuild the shattered communities in the cities which had been bombed into rubble during the war years. Uncontrolled development was a very real threat and the coming into force of the Town and Country Planning (Scotland) Act 1947 laid the ground rules for what was to be the building, rebuilding and modernisation of Britain's housing.

Permits were required to buy certain materials and one of these was wood. Only a certain amount was permitted per property and usually only enough to construct either the floors, ceilings, *or* partitions. Mr Hastings was therefore somewhat less than pleased when we came to inspect one house at Dunrossness which had beautiful timber walls and floors, even the loft was lined and floored. "Where did you get all this wood?" he asked.

"Fae da sea," was the answer.

Both during the war and afterwards, huge cargoes of wood were lost from ships which were sunk, or was swept overboard from deck cargoes in bad weather. Every kind of wood was washed ashore from pit-props to beautiful deals of hardwood and when 'saved' was either 'laid up' above high-water mark at the head of the beach or taken home and stored in a shed. In either case it was sacrosanct as no one would have thought of taking another person's wood. Some of it, I am sure, is still there to this day, overgrown with grass or still in the 'roof trees' of old buildings. In this particular case, however, as the person was an excellent craftsman and had made really worthwhile use of his 'winnings', no further action was taken.

The word 'sanitary' in the title of the post is something of a misnomer in that, although the prime role of the inspector is to ensure and promote the health and wellbeing of the community, his duties also cover a multitude of other tasks. In 1949, and for many years afterwards, there were no separate housing or planning departments. Housing, in all its different guises from overcrowding to allocations to improvement grants, was a function of the sanitary department and planning was controlled by comments on each application from the sanitary, roads' and architect's departments, collated and reported to the general purposes committee by Annie Halcrow at the County Buildings. I can remember that, when we were eventually granted a five-day-week, Annie insisted on going to the office on Saturday mornings as she had always done so and would not change.

The county clerk was the perennial John N. Sinclair, who was never known to take a holiday. The other mainstays at the County Buildings were Willie Clark and Benny Manson ('Bill and Ben, the coonty clerk's men'). The finance department was run by Jim Leask who walked around with his glasses hanging from one ear! He was ably assisted by 'Peerie Frankie' Sinclair, Hamish Leask, George Pottinger, Alec Munro and a few others. I still think that the preferable set-up was when each department had a recognisable 'head' and reported to a separate committee, all subservient to the eventual decision of the County Council. There have been many reorganisations over the years and I am not convinced that things are in any way improved.

It took me some time to learn the different functions of the other departments, and at the same time Mr Hastings was guiding me into the practical implications of the profession which I had chosen – and there were many practical implications such as pushing through rows of tightly packed sheep carcases to do meat inspection in antiquated and tiny slaughterhouses, and crawling in a drain track to test the integrity of the old fireclay pipes which were jointed with rope and cement and tested with a 'smoke box'. Sometimes, after the workers got to know me, I would find that a balloon had been put into the drain about a couple of feet from the end so that was the extent of what I was testing, and some of them, like Bertie Burgess in Scalloway, had rather more descriptive titles for me than the official one.

CHAPTER EIGHT

Theory and Practice

A FTER a year, I was ready to begin my course of study at Heriot-Watt College in Chambers' Street, Edinburgh. I was very lucky to be able to find accommodation with a Shetland couple: Jimmy Smith from Bressay, his wife Minna and their daughters, Annette and Bettina (now the wife of Dr Gavin Strang), who lived in Restalrig Road, Leith. This is, of course, the area of Leith which is, or was, populated by Shetland seamen who had 'slung their hook' and settled down, many with jobs at the docks. I was the first student they had accommodated, but I was able to fit in with the household from the start.

Although I was nominally here only for classes at the college, these were only on one day and a few evenings in the week, so an arrangement had been made with the Edinburgh City Council public health department that I would be able to gain work experience, albeit unpaid, when I was not at the college. This, again, like my time in the RAF, was a real education for life as it took me into the darkest and (at that time) most deprived areas of the city.

The public health department was in Johnstone Terrace, more-or-less at the back of Edinburgh Castle. When I reported there I was allocated to an inspector, Bill Jackson, who would be responsible for 'showing me the ropes' and guiding me during my four years at the college. One day I was called to the office of the depute medical officer of health for Edinburgh which was on the floor above our office. When I arrived there I saw that the name on the door was 'Dr Mair' and on entering was amazed to find that this was one of the 'Holmsgarth Mairs', with the nickname 'Tibby', a contemporary of my brother Jim, and uncle of the two Mairs from my Class 10 in the Central.

Having discovered my presence in the building he had made a point of making contact so as to get up-to-date news of family and home.

I also discovered that there were two other apprentices who had arrived on the same footing as myself, one from Thurso and one from Wick. We soon realised that we had an inordinate amount of free time from the college with only two evenings and one afternoon at classes and, unlike the other local students on the course, we could not get home other than at the end of each term. Together we approached the head of studies to see if our course could be compressed into three years instead of four. This would mean that we would have lectures every evening and one day, but we were willing to accept this with a view to finishing earlier and getting back home. He was very understanding and actually spent a great deal of time working out a special timetable just to suit our requirements.

So, operating from Johnstone Terrace virtually every day, I spent the winter of 1950/51 in tenements, shops, slums, decrepit housing estates and even very expensive town houses in the new town where rats were so ill-mannered as to appear. One visit which I vividly remember was to an old lady who occupied a 'single-end' in a very old building at the foot of the Canongate, I think formerly a stable, at Whitehorse Close, opposite Holyrood Palace. She had complained about rats and when I visited her and asked whether there were any she replied, "Rats as big as bloody doags, mister, running ower ma bed at night." I duly set some traps and, although not perhaps of the dimensions suggested, she certainly had rats in abundance, which we were able to remove for a time at least.

At that time the department was also involved in the first trials in UK of the new anticoagulant rat-poison called 'warfarin'. The sites chosen were the basements of premises in Leith Street, just off Princes Street – I am stressing the basement as the upper floors were rumoured to be houses of ill-repute and we apprentices were chaperoned by qualified staff whenever we went to that area! During the experiments it was found that, in the first instance, only old and decrepit rats approached the bait and when they appeared to be unaffected the others ate it without fear. As the warfarin took several days to take effect, all the generations of rats would have hopefully eaten their fill before the effects, which were invariably fatal, began. It is somewhat ironic that several of my friends are now regularly ordering supplies of this stuff to keep them alive!

The staff at Johnstone Terrace, from the bosses to the secretaries, were a very friendly and helpful crowd and we 'Northerners' were soon very much at home. Every morning we had to report at 9am and write up the visits and action which had been carried out the previous day, then receive instructions and be told the programme for the day. We also were given 'tokens', a strictly controlled amount, to pay the conductors on the trams and buses (at that time it was about 4d from Corstorphine to Joppa at Portobello). Then everyone went their own way – officially – but at 10.30am the vast majority of the inspectors could be found in Crawford's Tea Rooms at the foot of the 'Bridges' having coffee. To be honest, this was not an everyday occurrence and it did not take a lot of time, but was a very good way of being able to exchange information about certain clients and properties outwith the walls of the office.

Then it was into the fray, arguments about whose turn it was to wash the tenement stairs, was the barman putting water in the whisky, rats and mice, petty tenancy arguments which needed the 'Sanitry' to sort out, all in the very interesting day's work! On Wednesdays there were classes in meat inspection which entailed attendance at the huge slaughterhouse in Gorgie Road. Incidentally, the slaughterhouse had been built back-to-front, with all the big windows in the roof facing south instead of north.

As I have said, there were classes almost every evening and it took a great deal of time to write up the notes afterwards. My writing is notoriously bad so I really had to concentrate to make legible the scribbles which were produced during the lectures. At this point I shall interject a story which involves Meg at a much later stage. While teaching a primary 7 class at the Central School she was having difficulty with one pupil in that his writing was so bad that she had to call on the headmaster, George W. Blance to "have a word". He discussed the problem with Meg and then told her his story: "Once upon a time there were three boys in the control class and I threatened not to allow them to sit the control exam unless their writing improved. Their names were Douglas Smith, Douglas Conochie and Ian Fraser." With that he turned and left the room. (By then I was county sanitary inspector, Douglas Conochie was an educational psychologist and Ian Fraser was headmaster at Scalloway School!)

I seem to recall that we were given time-off at the office to pursue our studies and this must have been the case as my method of 'swotting' was to write everything down so often that I could remember it 'parrotwise' and, if I knew that an answer required one and a bit pages of foolscap and I had not achieved this, something was missing. Part of our course was the first three years of the architect's course involving a great deal of highly technical and detailed drawing which I really enjoyed and that stood me in good stead when I eventually qualified and began work back home again

There were relaxations of course. Every Saturday one went either to Easter Road or Tynecastle to watch the football. These were the years when the Hibs' 'famous five' – Smith, Johnstone, Reilly, Turnbull and Ormond – were in full swing, as were Conn, 'King Willie' Bauld and Wardhaugh at Hearts.

Although I was alone in the digs at this stage, there were many friends not far away. Ian Fraser, Alec Thompson and Bertie Laurenson were in digs with another Shetland couple in Summerfield Terrace, just a few hundred yards away, and we met up when time permitted. The Shetland Association held dances from time to time in the Assembly Rooms in Constitution Street, Leith, and these were excellent venues for meeting up with the other exiles. There was also the Orkney and Zetland Association which held functions at their rooms in Hill Street, but we always considered them rather too 'up-market' for students.

So, soon it was time for exams and then back home for the six months practical period in Shetland. This system was really invaluable as I was getting practical experience in both city and county environments, both completely different and yet controlled by the same laws.

Being a bit more conversant with the legal requirements of the job, I was able to do more duties on my own, but only when authorised and clearly instructed by Mr Hastings. As I could not drive, a taxi had to be ordered and fairly often this was driven by 'Old Johnnie' Leask, the founder of the firm, John Leask & Son. Preparations were being made for the provision of a programme of water schemes in various districts of Shetland and water samples had to be taken from all the lochs which would be used as sources.

When we went to Yell and Unst we took Mr Hastings' car to Mossbank, then hired the small ferry over to Ulsta, hired a car from there to Gutcher, hired the boat across to Belmont and then another taxi in Unst. Stories of these journeys would fill another book so I shall restrict my comments to one about the driver in Yell who used to switch off the engine whenever we came to an incline and coast down to the bottom to save fuel (I am sure that he had a spirit-level somewhere on the dashboard). This may have saved fuel, but we also took an hour and a quarter to cross Yell! At the end of a working day I was often offered a dram (steadfastly refused) before I set off home, and I can well remember a lady in Unst asking if I would like 'a refreshment', or would I rather have beer!

Whalsay was another unique situation. This is, of course, before the car ferries existed and the *Earl of Zetland* went as far as Uyeasound and back on Wednesdays, stopping at Symbister in both directions. This gave us a more-or-less full day in the 'Bonnie Isle', where our contact was Johnnie Anderson, of Anderson's Battery Services and much more. Johnnie knew what was going

'Whalsay Willie', Frances Taylor, me and Mr Hastings, waiting for the Earl *at Symbister.*

on in the island and if we 'phoned and told him where we thought we should visit he could suggest that there was no need to come for a week or so as some of the necessary materials had not yet arrived. I can well remember trying to phone Johnnie on Symbister 15, via the manned exchange which was at Gardenstown, only to be told, "You needna' try dem, dere a' hill!" which translated into the fact that he and family were not at home but working in the peat hill. On another occasion I was taking a water sample from a tap in Johnnie Anderson's house. In order to sterilise the tap I used the burner for a Tilley lamp soaked in methylated spirits to flame the end of the tap. Suddenly, I was aware of a small figure behind me, poking at my leg and saying, "Bad unkan man, burnin' daddy's tap." In the interest of a quiet life I will not identify the child. Another event enjoyed/endured during Whalsay trips were the journeys over to Billister in Nesting on the flitboat *Shearwater* with 'Muckle Peter', a man of infinite vocabulary, especially when a wave broke over him!

There are far too many stories about the *Earl* and her exploits over the years to list them all, but I really think that I must include at least a couple. It was normally the case that the *Earl*, which normally only sailed between Lerwick and Baltasound, went to Aberdeen for annual refit in January, and the students returning to university had to endure the passage on the relatively small vessel in the worst part of the winter. It was also the case that at nine o'clock at night the captains of the various 'north boats' would speak to one another on the radio. It is said that, on one trip when the *Earl* was heading for Aberdeen, a call was received from Captain Andrew Ramsay on the *St Ninian*. This was duly answered, "*St Ninian, Earl of Zetland* calling." Captain Ramsay then responded, "Is yun da *Earl* – da peerie *Earl*. What are you doin' oot here i' da dark?"

Captain Willie Sinclair of the *Earl* was also a great entertainer and I can remember approaching Lerwick from the north one summer afternoon with Willie on the bridge and a crowd of tourists on deck. The captain was giving his instructions to the helmsman roughly as follows, "Steer Magnie Shearer's lum over the Town Hall clock," and the man at the wheel responding with a straight face, "Magnie Shearer's lum over the Town Hall clock it is, sir." The tourists were duly impressed as the course was changed.

Happy days, no mobiles, although they would have been a real bonus on some occasions when one had just returned from some extremity to find that another request for a visit had arrived in the meantime for the same area. In any event, the summer passed and soon it was back to Edinburgh and 'The Watt'. The main change, for me at least, during the second year was that I was joined at the digs by Kenny Groat. I had obviously known Kenny for many years and he was an ideal companion. There was no 'binge drinking' in those days, usually a pint at the 'Greyfriars Bobby' pub on Friday evening after classes *or* on Saturday after the football was the height of our excesses. There was one occasion, however, when we might have broken our routine in that we always filled in the football coupon with a five-shilling (25p) bet. One Saturday we checked the results and found that we had 23 out of the possible 24 points. Being now potential millionaires we invited a couple of pals for a pint in the 'Cricketers Arms', opposite the digs. On Monday we were glad that we had not taken the matter further as we discovered that several thousands of others had also got 23 points and the pay-out was 2/6 (12½p).

Most of the classes were progressions from the previous year, and some new, but the routine was obviously very similar each year. During the final year I once again made contact with the Rev Courtland Smith who had moved his charge to Currie on the outskirts of Edinburgh. Several of the Shetland students occasionally attended his evening services, and were always invited to the barn dances which he organised in the church hall. Lifts back to the city were by private car, often driven by Alex or George Buchanan-Smith, members of a prominent local family.

So on to the end of the final year, March 1953, when we sat our final exams at the college, and also the examination of the Royal Sanitary Association of Scotland to be accepted as a qualified sanitary inspector. Having successfully overcome all the hurdles I arrived home to advise the county clerk that I had fulfilled the requirements of the 'Articles of Apprenticeship' and, on 19th May, 1953, I was appointed as qualified assistant in the county sanitary inspector's department at an annual salary of £520 rising by annual increments of £15 to £565. I had made it but, as with driving a car, it is only after one has passed the driving test that one really learns how to drive!

And, talking of driving, I got my first provisional licence in 1953 and had various 'shots' of the Conochie's car and others but never had any 'real' tuition, and merely succeeded in failing my test, quite understandably. Then Meg decided that she was the one to help me pass my test as she had been driving her father's car for years. In the interim, of course, we had become engaged at Christmas-time, 1949, so I was now duty bound to obey every instruction, and pass I did on the 14th June, 1954. By then I had bought our first car, RG6667, a 1935 Hillman Coupe with a canvas roof and aluminium body, wooden wheel-arches and big brass hinges everywhere.

In 1953, having been engaged to Meg for almost four years and having qualified and been appointed to a post with a regular salary, the time seemed appropriate to think about getting married. There were various considerations to be taken into account, one of those being that Meg's sister, Marie, and her fiancée, Wally Emmott, were also of the same opinion. Wally had been at Sumburgh for some time, employed by the Civil Aviation Authority at the installation on top of Compass Head, immediately above Grutness. This

Happy days, Grutness, 1953.

Jim and Mary Ann Black, Grutness, 1978.

Wedding Day, 30th September, 1953.

Wally and me, relaxing!

suggested that a double wedding would be the most sensible outcome. However, Wally's home was in Preston and his parents were unable to travel to Shetland, so the decision was made that the wedding would be on 30th September, 1953, at Pilrig Church, Edinburgh. Edinburgh was chosen as it was an easy place to reach for most relatives, including Wally's, who would want to attend, and also because both Meg and I had been students there (Meg at Moray House in the Canongate and living in Buchanan Hostel in East Suffolk Road, Newington). Pilrig Church because the minister was the Rev James Robertson, a Shetlander who had been a pupil of both my aunt Daisy at the Central and my mother at the Institute.

The great day duly arrived and went, and we prepared to go on honeymoon. Wally and Marie set off for Palma while Meg and I were bound for Jersey. However, just before we left home for Edinburgh, we had received a letter from the hotel proprietors in Jersey to say that the hotel was closing down in October but we could stay as '*en familie*' if that was suitable. We thought that this was not what we wanted so the manager of the Royal British Hotel ('RB') in Princes Street, where the reception was held, contacted a friend in London and arranged accommodation for us in the Milestone Hotel in Kensington, London. This hotel actually has an ancient milestone at the front door, indicating one mile from the centre of London. This was a very pleasant small hotel and we walked all over the centre of London. This was 1953 and many bombed sites were still very much in evidence. I particularly remember Fleet Street where there was willow herb blooming in profusion amongst the shattered walls and debris. Being in London also gave us the chance to visit aunty Mary, uncle Alec and Jean at Glendoone.

Then it was time to head north again and to begin married life in '55', me back at the office and Meg teaching at the Central. As I have said already, '55' was a very awkward house, with our bedroom on the top floor, the bathroom on the middle floor, and the kitchen and living room on the first floor, steps everywhere, and sharing this with my mother was never an ideal solution, but there was obviously room in the house for both families.

Grutness House.

Changes

B ACK in the office, big changes were afoot. The youth employment service had been combined with the education department who needed more room, and it was decided that our department would move to the 'House of David' at 92 St Olaf Street. It had been utilised as flats, the families gradually being re-housed, and the council had bought the building which was the first mass concrete house to be built in Lerwick. It was also innovative in that there was a long-out-of-use built-in system of ducts which fed hot air from a source on the ground floor to the rooms on the two floors above.

Now converted to offices (including the use of a compressor to cut doors in the very solid internal walls), the building now housed the county assessor's department on the ground floor, the county sanitary inspector's department and the architect's clerks of works on the first floor and the county architect's department on the second floor. Much internal work was required in our general office, including the provision of a counter at the access door for the public. The two joiners who arrived to build the counter were none other than Aly Bain and his father.

Over the years between 1953 and 1974 (when the department moved to 3 Commercial Road) these offices met the needs of the staff which grew from three – Mr Hastings, myself and a secretary – as additional legislation placed more responsibility on the department. This was particularly so in the case of food hygiene, and milk and dairies, where more and more emphasis was being placed on cleanliness, refrigeration and sampling. This was added to by the ever increasing number of applications to build new houses and the modernisation of old properties.

In the interim, however, Mr Hastings and I enforced the legislation as best we could. Being a local it was sometimes a bit awkward for me, when visiting someone north of Mavis Grind who was probably a relative of myself, or in the South Mainland who was likely to be a relative of Meg. However, I must say that there were never any problems on that score during the many years and countless times that the situation arose.

Times had moved on for friends as well and, for example, Freddy Tait was now a pilot with BOAC, flying huge aircraft to such exotic places as Japan. His sense of humour had not left him however, and on one occasion Mr Hastings was none too pleased when I received a postcard at the office from the Imperial Hotel, Tokyo, addressed only to 'Douglas Smith, The Insanitary Spectre, Lerwick', and signed 'Well-wisher'. It reached me and I had little problem guessing the perpetrator!

To give some idea of the different scale of things, when I began work there were actually no fewer than 56 dairy farms in Shetland, from Sumburgh to Unst, producing and selling milk and, apart from that, almost every crofter had his or her own cow. There were six milk shops in Lerwick – Ganson's dairy in Harbour Street, Lewis Moncrieff's in Burgess Street, Brucefield dairy in Thorfinn Street, Hoversta dairy in the Tolbooth, Bertie Smith's dairy in Commercial Road and Seaview Stores on Commercial Street. One amusing story concerns the antics of a shopkeeper in later years when the law insisted on all milk being cooled before being sold. I arrived to take a sample to find a pail of cooled milk being warmed over a primus stove in the backshop. When I enquired as to the reason, he said that folk would not know it was really 'moarnin's milk' unless it was warm.

Having just read in *The Shetland Times* that the last butcher shop on Commercial Street has closed, I think that it is worthy of note that not so long ago there were seven on the same street, Peterson & Co., Smith & Co., Peter Barclay, Lerwick Meat Co., Willie Lobban, Coop, and James S. Smith.

Slaughterhouses were spread throughout the county, including Hillswick, Mossbank, Voe, Weisdale, Vementry, Scalloway, Lerwick, Sandwick, Boddam, Burra Isle, Whalsay, Mid Yell, and Baltasound, and later Stump Farm at

Reawick (these, however, were by no means all the places in which animals were being slaughtered). Now there are only two.

Public drainage schemes formerly existed only in Lerwick and Scalloway but this had risen to 20 areas by 1986. From two public water supply schemes (also in Lerwick and Scalloway) the total rose to 29 by 1986. All these increases required a huge amount of travelling time for inspections and sampling, but this was greatly eased with the introduction of the vehicle ferries to the north isles. The provision of piped supplies of water also provided a great boost to the improvement in housing conditions throughout the islands. But more stringent water quality requirements and treatment facilities have led to a huge reduction, as more and more of the 29 smaller schemes were linked to the major supply sources at Eelawater in Northmavine, and the Sandy Loch, near Lerwick, both provided with sophisticated treatment works. These two now supply the vast majority of houses on the mainland of Shetland.

Housing grants for housing improvement were only beginning to be considered and, in 1949, a total of nine were approved with a maximum grant of £600. There was a massive increase over the ensuing years and consequent dramatic improvement in housing standards in the county.

I mentioned earlier that the studies into architectural drawing undertaken during the three years at Heriot-Watt were put to good use later. Mr Hastings decided that the best way to obtain compliance with legislation was for plans to be prepared in the department for each of the dairies, slaughterhouses, etc., where work was required. These were then taken to the premises and shown to the proprietors as being the minimum upheaval required to comply with the legislation which would allow them to continue in their trade. Needless to say, the task of preparing the plans was handed to me, and I can still identify a considerable number of buildings in the county which originated on my drawing board in 92 St Olaf Street. I hasten to add that, as these were being produced during working hours, there was never any charge made!

However, as bacteriological and chemical standards became more and more stringent, many premises gave up food production but those which were left required more and more supervision.

One change to the duties of Mr Hastings occurred in 1954 when the burgh surveyor for Lerwick retired. The Town Council decided to appoint an engineer as surveyor but he was not qualified to be burgh sanitary inspector, so Mr Hastings was approached to undertake the duties of burgh, as well as county, sanitary inspector. Although many of the duties are governed by similar legislation, the practical implications are quite different, particularly referring to the tightly packed housing in the lanes of the burgh compared to the scattered nature of the communities in the county.

There was also the occasional problem with the 'tinker' families who occupied buses and tents in a quarry at the roadside between where the Marts is now situated and the former Decca Station on the old North Road. The 'matriarch', old Mrs MacPhee, lived on her own in the concrete shelter at the side of the road leading up the Staney Hill from the Clickimin Centre. In the main the problems were of a medical nature, but I was often sent to report on conditions to Dr Black. Despite being offered houses from time to time, these folk preferred their very rough lifestyle and persisted in refusing help. The only ones who settled in permanent housing at that time were Peter and Nelly Newlands. For many years Nelly was a 'weel kent' figure as she did her rounds throughout Shetland with her huge and very heavy pack slung over one shoulder.

Enforcement of legislation to improve hygienic standards in milk and water supplies was also causing much additional work, and Mr Hastings decided to seek permission to employ a milk officer. This was duly granted and the staff of the department, including the secretary, rose to four.

One routine which Mr Hastings insisted on following was the taking of samples of meat, under food and drugs legislation, annually on the second week of December. These samples were to check on the amount, if any, of preservatives being added to the product, this being very strictly controlled. There is a statutory procedure which has to be followed, and while this may be able to be undertaken in a sort of anonymous way in a city, the appearance of Mr Hastings and myself in a butcher shop in Lerwick during the second week of December, year after year, carrying a small suitcase, may have given a clue that we were not merely shopping for our evening meal! The procedure which had to be followed was that the shopkeeper had to be asked for, say, three-quarters of a pound of saucermeat. When this had been handed over and paid for, Mr Hastings had to tell the vendor that this had been purchased for the purpose of analysis and the sample would be divided into three parts and sealed in individual containers, one part being left with the vendor, one kept in our office in case of legal proceedings, and one sent to the public analyst for analysis. On one particular occasion we went into a shop and saw a tray with some saucermeat on the shelf behind the counter. Mr Hastings asked for the necessary three-quarters of a pound but the butcher, knowing perfectly well what was happening, said that this was old stuff and he would make a new batch. However, Mr Hastings insisted that it was on show and therefore available for sale so, having listened to the rest of the preamble, the butcher, Mr Peter Barclay of course, solemnly intoned, "And may God have mercy on your soul," – so much for anonymity! In any event the sample was 'genuine'. The need for preservative, or 'pinkie', was removed with the installation of refrigerated counters which transformed working and hygienic conditions in many shops.

There was another sea adventure which took place during this period. A new extension was being built in Fair Isle for the district nurse and a load of building materials, including concrete blocks, was to be carried there on the council workboat *Margaret Shearer*. It was decided that Mr Hasting, myself and Jock Henderson, a clerk of works, would travel as passengers and carry out inspections in 'the isle'. A former fishing boat, the *Margaret Shearer* was down to the Plimsoll line and had never carried such a weight for years. However, we set off from Lerwick early one morning, the weather was not too bad but certainly not calm, and by the time we were passing Mousa the engine-operated bilge pump became choked and the crew began to pump regularly with the hand pump. There was one slight problem with overall command. The skipper was from Whalsay and had never been to Fair Isle, so a skipper from Scalloway who knew the area well had been asked to accompany us as pilot. No Whalsa' skipper was going to turn back under the gaze of a Scallowa' man because of 'a corn a' sea' and vice-versa so we wallowed on. When we eventually arrived at the North Haven, hours later, we were told that the lighthouse keepers at Sumburgh Head and Fair Isle had been keeping a very close watch on our progress, fully expecting to have to call out the emergency services! We came back to Grutness on the *Good Shepherd*.

CHAPTER TEN

1955 – 64

AWAY from the office, 1955 was a very different year for both Mr Hastings and I. He and his wife had first lived in Annsbrae House in Lerwick but four semi-detached blocks of 'Swedish' houses had been built at Baila, on the outskirts of Lerwick but still in the county of Zetland. These were part of a programme of 40 Swedish houses which were built between 1947 and 1949 at Sandwick, Weisdale, Mossbank, Burravoe and Baila. The first four houses at Baila were allocated to local applicants while the remaining four were built for, and allocated to, county officials. Number 5 Baila was occupied by the county architect, Mr Conway; 6 Baila by the county assessor, Mr 'Ike' Gray; 7 Baila by the county sanitary inspector, Mr Hastings; and 8 Baila by the county road surveyor, Mr Dryburgh.

On 6th July, 1955, Mrs Hastings gave birth to a son, Ian, in the maternity annexe at Midgarth. Sadly and tragically, Mrs Hastings died on the 19th July, not having ever left the annexe. In time, once he had come to terms with his loss, Mr Hastings felt unable to continue living in the erstwhile family home at Baila and was allocated a house in Lerwick. In due course he re-married a family friend and Ian grew up and was educated here. (Having worked for, and been in the company of William L. Hastings for fifteen years, I invariably visualise his walk and mannerisms every time I see Ian.)

This was a very sad period but life, and work, had to go on. It was also particularly unfortunate that this happened while Meg was pregnant, expecting our first child in five months time. Mercifully, all went well and Gordon Arthur James Smith appeared on 2nd December, 1955, in the maternity annexe at Midgarth. (I still maintain that the name 'Gordon' had nothing to do with the fact that I was a Hibs supporter.) Twenty-one months later, Richard Burgess Campbell Smith was born and, coincidentally, I was elected to the Up-Helly-A' committee – the news not received with universal acclaim! In those days one had to phone the maternity annexe to report imminent arrivals, so when Meg indicated that things were moving I telephoned the exchange, which was still manned in those days, and asked to be connected to the annexe. Geordie Mundie was the operator that evening and his response was, "Again, Duggie?"

Apart from this, my father had become rather infirm through lumbago (whatever became of lumbago?), so had to give up his time at the office in Peterhead. I went down to bring him home as he was really unable for the boat journey and worried about flying. Actually, the last time he had been on a 'plane was, I think, 1937, when he was Provincial Grand Master of Morton Lodge, the local masonic organisation, and my mother and I joined him on the trip to Orkney which was in connection with the laying of the foundation stone of a new lodge at Longhope. Whatever the year, I can remember that in the hotel in Kirkwall there was a wind-up gramophone and one record, 'Easter Parade'. Anyway, I got some form of tranquillisers from his doctor in Peterhead which reduced his anxiety somewhat and we arrived home safely.

Meg and I were still living at 55 King Harald Street, but with two very small children the problems of the flights of stairs, carrying water etc., were beginning to put a severe strain on both households. This was now exacerbated by the permanent homecoming of dad, and we felt that the time had come for me to approach the Town Council for the allocation of a house. Now we came upon an impasse in that, because I was employed by the county, the Town Council would not consider our application, and the County Council would not grant us a tenancy because we were living in the burgh.

When Mr Hastings moved to Lerwick in 1953, the house which had been provided for the county sanitary inspector was then allocated to a tenant, Geoffrey Isodore de Mercado, and his wife and family. Geoff was a very talented classical violinist and a very keen etymologist and became very well known in Shetland. His wife was of African origin and, I think I may be permitted to say, slightly eccentric. In any event, early in 1958 they separated and the house was vacated. I then made a new application as this was the house which, to a certain extent 'belonged' to the department in which I was employed. In the spring of 1958 I was allocated the tenancy of 7 Baila, Sound, the tenancy to be accepted on the understanding that any work required to make the premises habitable had to be undertaken at my expense.

When Meg and I went to have a look at the house we got a bit of a shock. Geoffrey, through his work at the Meteorological Observatory, had fallen heir to some paint which was RAF blue in colour. Mrs Mercado had decided that this was the ideal colour scheme for the house and virtually everything had been painted blue, several walls, the complete staircase, bath, cooker and, believe it or not, the budgie's cage with the bird still inside, so that when it was allowed out there were blue flecks left on the ceiling of the living room. This was obviously going to take some time, but we persevered with help from some friends and moved in to our own first home. The 'flittin' was, in the main, carried out using the car, carrying as much as possible, including Gordon, while Meg pushed Richard out the road in the big Silver Cross pram.

Being, as they say, a bit 'cash strapped' and having virtually no furniture, we were dependent on the generosity of parents and friends to get us settled in and Meg still remembers that she dyed sheets to make curtains. Being a very competent seamstress she also made almost all the furnishings as well as the children's clothes so she had a real struggle, but her input allowed us to make ends meet – likely still does!

Baila at that time was not in the centre of the Sound community, as it is today. It was an isolated scheme of eight houses a long way from Lerwick and any shops. I suppose that, apart from Jean Jamieson and Peter and Lizzie Leask at Baila, the Malcolmsons' houses at Upper Sound were the nearest to us, but they were out of sight round the Baila corner. Looking towards Lerwick, the first house beside the road was that of Tammy Slater, near Clickimin Broch, and then one had to face the waves coming over the low sea wall at the ayre of Clickimin when the weather was bad, before coming to the 'Matchbox'. Helendale House was along the guttery road on the west side of the loch, and there were the original houses at Kantersted, Lower Sound and at the Sands of Sound. The main road was not the wide sweeping curve one sees now at Baila.

Instead, there was a sharp left hand turn below the Baila croft and along the front of the Swedish houses, which mercifully had a pavement in front. But this was the only pavement until one reached South Lochside on the east side of Clickimin Loch.

We had an excellent open view through the large window in the sitting room, and every evening, summer and winter, we would see Jean Jamieson going to visit her sheep. I purposely say 'visit' for these were her 'family'. If they were to be fed, she carried a huge bag of hay on her back. If it was after dark, she had a pocket torch which she shone on each one in turn, all this in the grassy fields where the Sound School complex now stands.

I was of course at work all day, five and a half days a week, and Meg had everything to do at home as well as entertaining the two lively young boys. One benefit which the residents of Sound do not have these days was the daily milk delivery by Irene Leask from Gulberwick, or weekly visits by Donnie Shewan from Quarff in his Landrover filled with vegetables, and for eggs we just had to go a few yards to Lizzie Leask at the original Baila croft. There was, of course, also the indispensable Co-op van driven by Joe Strachan and others. One of the first ambitions of the boys was to be a Co-op van driver which, certainly in part, proved to be somewhat prophetic in one case, as you will learn! Later Jimmy Fraser moved into 8 Baila with Lil, so a ready supply of fresh fish was immediately at hand!

While on the subject of fish, I was at this time undertaking another rather unusual project in my spare time. Beginning in the winter of 1958, fleets of small black vessels began to appear in the bays and voes on the east side of Shetland, particularly in the Fetlar area. These small vessels, which were soon identified as Russian trawlers, were accompanied by huge 'mother ships' and ancillary craft such as water tankers and tugs. As the years progressed these fleets grew in size to several hundreds of vessels and their lights resembled floating towns in the hours of darkness.

The water tankers began to come to Lerwick on a regular basis to load with water for drinking purposes and for use in the processing plants on the factory ships. A few inquisitive Lerwegians, including myself, used to go down to the Albert Quay where the tankers often lay, in the first instance because we always had an interest in any form of shipping in the harbour, but the main reason was because the Cold War was still very much in evidence and even being able to *see* a Russian at such close quarters was really almost unique in the west. At first they were very suspicious, always under the eye of a political officer, but as time passed and they began to recognise us and realise that we were not going to cause problems they began to relax.

Obviously there was a huge language problem. Nobody in Shetland could speak Russian at that time (or owned up to being able) and only the very occasional Russian captain who had sailed deep-sea in their merchant navy had anything approaching a reasonable command of English (or owned up to being able). It was very noticeable in the early stages that whenever any of us were attempting to speak to one of the crew an official-looking uniformed person would be standing well within earshot, just in case something suspicious was under discussion, and as time progressed, if a question was asked, it was always the 'politico' who would answer.

My cousin, Alec Campbell, was a chemist and his shop was frequented by the medical personnel to get medicines and first-aid equipment for their sick-bays. In this way he began to get invited on board the boats and I sometimes accompanied him, together with the local shipping agent, Andy Beattie from Messrs Hay & Co. We began to be able to exchange a few words in each other's languages and I decided to try to learn a bit more as there was no interpreter in Shetland at the time. The importance of having more than just a rudimentary understanding of the Russian language, and their pronunciation of English, can be illustrated by the following tale.

A Russian skipper had been visiting Alec and his wife, Rita, at their home at Midgarth in Twageos Road. On the way back to the ship via Commercial Street, Alec was somewhat thunderstruck when the skipper asked him if he would help him pay for a prostitute! Not being aware of any houses of doubtful repute in the town, Alec asked in what way he was expected to help. The skipper replied that he had seen one in a shop on the street, but the shop was shut! This left Alec more baffled than ever, and this was compounded when, passing Laurenson Bros, the gents' outfitters (now Smith's of Lerwick), the skipper stopped and said, "There!" Having known the staff of the premises for many years, Alec thought that there must be some mistake and this was confirmed when the skipper pointed to a model in the window and said, "There it is!" The object of his desire was in fact a PLASTIC COAT!

I have always been interested in languages and, having achieved higher French and lower Latin during my six years at the Institute, I began to study a 'Teach Yourself Russian' course. To my surprise and delight I realised that Russian grammar is almost exactly the same as Latin, and I soon learned the 32 letters of the alphabet but there was always the problem of pronunciation, many Russian words having completely different meanings depending on where the accent is placed. I then discovered that there was a 'Russian by Radio' course being broadcast by Radio Moscow, once a week. I wrote to the station and was sent the test papers which I completed and sent back each week, the main problem being that it took two weeks for the corrected entries to be returned and by that time I had usually memorised the wrong words in the interim! As an aside, I discovered that the tutor was the man who had been interpreter for Yuri Gagarin, the first man in space, when he visited Britain. We also discovered that we were both keen philatelists and exchanged many stamps, although I must say that the Russian issues were, at that time, much more artistic than our own.

Meg, usually the instigator of any permanent solution, suggested that I should attempt to get some form of qualification, rather than just working on my own, so I approached Wolsey Hall College, part of London University, with a view to studying for an 'O' level in Russian. This entailed a 26-week study course in the first year and 32 weeks in the second year. By now I had been working on my own for about four years so had an idea that I could perhaps escape the first few lessons on the course. I therefore asked the college to send me a test paper from some weeks into the first year. It arrived and the questions were, roughly speaking, as follows: *'Give the Present Participle Active and the Past Participle Passive of the following Perfect and Imperfect verbs......'*

I immediately went to John Graham, headmaster at the Institute and asked for the loan of an English primer, then wrote to Wolsey Hall College and asked for lesson No. 1!

I persevered with the course, trying to devote an hour per evening when time permitted, with the much appreciated help of Meg, who was pressurised into learning the Russian alphabet so that she could check my vocabularies. She can still say, "Ya ne govoru horosho po Russki." ("I don't speak Russian well.")

I sat the 'O' level exam in the education offices in Brentham Place under the watchful eye of A.K. Robertson, who had undertaken the Russian interpreter's course in the forces – unknown to anyone of course – and I passed, in January, 1963.

By now the Russians were regularly coming ashore and visiting the pubs and the picture house – perestroika at first hand. My particular friend was Captain Nikolai Borisevitch Tseitlin of the water tanker *Kartaly* from Murmansk. Nikolai was a native of Leningrad but had fought in Yugoslavia during the war and had a scar across the side of his face which gave him a somewhat 'handsome-gangsterish' appearance. His favourite haunt in Lerwick was the bar of the Grand Hotel and, if asked where he was bound for he would say, "I go see Djerry Pottinger," who was the barman at the time.

As the years passed the visits became fewer, and different ships replaced the old favourites, but on Christmas Eve, 1959, the 'phone at Baila rang. This was Hay & Company to say that Nikolai was in Lerwick and wanted to come and see us. I collected him with the car and it was quite strange to see the effect on him when he came into the living room where we had all the Christmas decorations, the tree, and lots of cards and wrapped presents. There were tears in his eyes when he said that he had never seen anything like this since he was a little boy. He then wanted to see our two boys, then aged four and two, who were asleep in bed upstairs. Meg took him up to the room and he lifted the bedclothes at the foot of the beds and kissed their feet. It was a very moving visit, real friendship instead of hate and suspicion from across the 'iron curtain'.

Meg was actually expecting another child at the time and as we drank a toast, Nikolai said, "You have two boys, this will be a girl." Then I took him back to the *Kartaly* which sailed next morning, after their final visit to Lerwick.

True to his predictions, Jill was born in May, so I wrote and told Nikolai the glad tidings and at Christmas, 1960, a parcel, sewn in canvas, arrived with the postmark 'Copenhagen'. This was a real Russian 'Ded Moroz' or 'Father Frost' figurine, which has stood in a prominent position every Christmas since then, firstly in our house, then was passed on to Jill. Nikolai and all the 'old gang' sailed away, never to return.

On one occasion I was actually asked to act as interpreter in a court case where a Russian trawler had been caught fishing inside the three mile limit off Sumburgh Head. The skipper claimed that he was fishing for scientific purposes, which was apparently permissible, but I refused to become involved in the legal process as, through my lack of ability, I could have influenced the outcome one way or another. An interpreter for the prosecution was therefore brought from England, and a second secretary from the Russian Embassy in London came to act for the defence. At the trial, the Russian skipper appeared to have great difficulty understanding the accent of the English interpreter and finally Sheriff Alistair MacDonald asked if the Russian interpreter would act for both sides! In the end the skipper was found guilty, but as this was the first case of its kind he was admonished, but the second secretary was strongly advised to inform all other fishing vessels frequenting this area to operate within the laws of this country or face the penalties.

This was not the end of the affair however as Andy Beattie, the shipping agent for the Russians, and I, had been asked to go to the Queens Hotel during the evening to meet the Russian second secretary, who produced a bottle of vodka from under his pillow and poured us a dram. He spoke perfect English so we raised the question of the Russian seamen who were beginning to become regular patients at the Gilbert Bain Hospital. At this time I seemed to be the only Russian speaking person in Lerwick who was called on to interpret at the hospital when injured seamen were landed for treatment. Initially suspicious, they soon realised that everyone concerned was trying to do their best, and many friendships grew, especially with those who were badly hurt and had to remain for treatment for an extended period. One was actually taught by the nurses to say, "I'm joost a poor aald boady," when asked how he was feeling!

Andy Beattie and I arranged for a box of books and a radio set to be sent to the hospital by the Soviet Embassy in London so that the patients could read or listen to the boats speaking on marine band. (I do not know what became of the books, but the radio set was 'nicked' by someone, which was disappointing.) Often the horizon, seen from the hospital, was obscured by the mass of boats of all sizes sheltering in Breiwick in all kinds of weather.

On our way back home along the street, Andy and I were stopped by the skipper of the Russian trawler who was window-shopping. This is hard to believe, but he then invited us to a party which was onboard the British fishery protection vessel lying at the fish market! Intrigued, we followed him and found a very congenial evening in progress which culminated in the captain of the naval ship presenting the Russian skipper with the ship's crest, and the Russian sending one of his crew to remove the Hammer and Sickle flag from the jackstaff which he then draped around the neck of the captain like a scarf! Maybe this was an early chink in the iron curtain, it certainly took place, and I can't imagine this happening anywhere other than in Shetland during that particular era.

About this time there was another example of cooperation between the west, in the shape of Shetland, and the Soviet Union which must have been unique. It had been a very dry summer and the water supply in the Out Skerries had virtually dried up. In addition, the harbour is very small and has a restricted entrance and there was no easy way of replenishing the small reservoir. It so happened that the Russian fleet had for some time been using a water tanker which had been converted from one of the trawlers, so was much smaller than the others. This vessel, the *Katcha*, was, providentially, small enough to get into the harbour at Skerries and, with the agreement of the Soviet authorities, made more than one trip from Lerwick fully laden with water which was pumped over into the reservoir and averted a potentially serious problem for the islanders. Arthur Tait of the council's water department had also by then grasped enough of the Russian language to hold a conversation, so occasionally there were some rather strange exchanges on the internal 'phone line between our departments.

One other rather unusual encounter was when John Smith of Shearer Shipping, by then the agent for the Russian fishing fleet, telephoned me with a request to translate a legal document which required to be lodged at the Sheriff Court within 24 hours. I replied that I would try, but could give no guarantee that I would get it finished in time or that it would be totally accurate in legal terms even if completed.

A Russian tug, the *Purga*, was lying at Victoria Pier and John took me on board to meet Captain Babak, who had prepared a statement of four typed pages of A4 to be translated. The situation was that the *Purga* had been towing a huge barge from Murmansk to a breaker's yard in the Baltic. When they were passing along the rocky and reef-strewn west coast of Norway, in the area of Florø, a violent storm blew up, the tow parted, and the barge was driven ashore and became a total loss. There is a legal process whereby Captain Babak had to lodge what is called a 'marine protest' stating his defence against any action which might be taken against him in relation to the stranding.

With the aid of my trusty dictionaries, and sitting with the captain sketching on paper the system of ropes, springs, bridles, hawse-holes and suchlike nautical technicalities not normally found in dictionaries, I was able to get a mental picture of what had happened. Back home, I then had to translate the remainder of the evidence and get it typed into understandable English. I can still remember that the final claim of the captain was that the cause was *force majeur*. I had refused to accept any payment for this work as, if I had through my translation (or mis-translation!) contributed in any way to a charge being proven in relation to the incident, I would no doubt have been caught up in the process and I had no wish for that.

Then the *Purga* sailed away and I heard no more of the incident. Believe it or not, her next port of call was Novorossiysk, on the west coast of the Black Sea. Her task was to collect a floating crane from there and tow it back to Murmansk – have a look at a map. In any event, months later, or so it seemed, I saw a strange silhouette on the horizon and as it approached I realised that this was a crane, in fact it was the crane being towed by the *Purga*, calling in at Lerwick for supplies on the last lap of her epic voyage! I went down and spoke to Captain Babak who had had no further approach for evidence from the authorities so presumably nothing more ever came of the incident.

My Russian capabilities were never adequate, certainly in relation to medical emergencies, although greatly assisted by the large and all-encompassing dictionaries which were given me by friends on the tankers. It was therefore a great relief (I am sure to all concerned) when Derrick Herning arrived at the Institute in 1967. Derick's fluency in a multitude of languages is quite mind-boggling, especially when conducting a conversation in several languages at the same time! Suffice to say that I was very happy to withdraw and operate on the sidelines.

My final link with the Soviet block was when the mother-ship *Darius* was marooned at Dales Voe for many months and I made friends with some of the crew, and increased my collection of beautiful Russian stamps. These friendships still continue and, as I am typing this, I have just had a telephone call from the wife of one of the crew who lives in Klaipeda – luckily she speaks perfect English as I have forgotten most of what Russian I learned. There are also a few Russian ladies married and living in Shetland just now, so I do get the chance to exchange the odd word now and again.

Jill Marguerite Smith, the first girl to be born into the 'Islesburgh Smith' family for 80 years, was born in the maternity annexe at Midgarth on 29th May, 1960, the morning after the 'Hamefarin' torchlight event at Clickimin Broch. So, now Meg had three under the age of five, and walks became a bit fraught, with Gordon charging ahead on his tricycle and Richard 'helping' to push Jill in the pushchair or pram. This was, as you will recall, on the main road with no pavements until they were able to turn off down the Helendale road which, to the delight of the boys at least, was often filled with potholes.

Gordon started school at Bell's Brae in 1960. I would deliver him, sometimes under protest, to Mrs Deyell or some other custodian and go to my work. At the end of the day Meg would have to collect him, with Richard and Jill in tow. There was no school transport, even to the Observatory where several families were in residence, so after having unsuccessfully petitioned the education authority for transport because of the unsafe nature of the road, a group of parents agreed to pay a small weekly charge each and a taxi was hired from Leask's. This arrangement lasted for years, bringing major peace of mind to the parents of the small children, until the bus service was introduced. I am sure that the driver of the taxi, often Jimmy Leask himself, had many an amusing moment as he witnessed (and overheard) the growing up of his small charges!

In 1960 Mr Hastings decided that the volume of work had increased to a stage where we could benefit from the addition of a qualified assistant. I was then upgraded to become depute county sanitary inspector in April 1963, with a salary of £930 per annum.

Winter visits to the isles sometimes caused problems, but maybe I was fortunate in that I can only remember two instances when Mr Hastings and I were storm-stayed. The first was in Whalsay, when the sea conditions were too rough for the *Earl* to anchor at Symbister (there was at that time no breakwater or pier at which to moor) and too rough for the flitboat to cross to Billister. We found accommodation with Mrs Sinclair in the big house, 'Brucefield', at the top of the brae near the hall. Warm and comfortable overnight, we were able to set off homewards in the morning after a very hearty breakfast.

The second time was in Yell very early in 1964. A very bad storm blew up while we were carrying out visits there so the ferry from Ulsta to Toft was cancelled. It was bitterly cold and we were both wet and thoroughly miserable. Mr Hastings contacted Mr Stove, the headmaster at Mid Yell with whom he was friendly, and arranged to spend the night there, while I made contact with Alec Thomson whom I had known since the days at the Institute, now a teacher, and was given a very comfy bed at Aywick. Next morning the weather was still bad but it eased sufficiently for us to cross Yell Sound later in the day.

This experience was to have more far-reaching implications than I could have anticipated. Mr Hastings developed a very bad cold which became more and more serious. Eventually he was hospitalised and, when his condition worsened, he was flown to the Royal Infirmary in Aberdeen where he died on 19th April, 1964. Having been in his company on a day-to-day basis for the past fifteen years this news came as a tremendous shock to me. My every move had been dictated and controlled by his instructions and according to his methods, so now the future was going to be very different, whatever the outcome.

The funeral of William L. Hastings was to take place in his home village of Airth, near Falkirk. Having been the employee most closely involved with Mr Hastings over the years, I approached the county clerk, John N. Sinclair, to ask whether I could represent the Zetland County Council at the funeral. There was actually a county council meeting on the day before the date of the funeral and at that meeting I was authorised to attend at Airth. Having anticipated a favourable decision, I had provisionally booked a seat on the 'plane and had packed a case, so I left the meeting, called along Baila to tell Meg, and went straight to Sumburgh. While I was waiting at the airport, the convener, Mr R.A. ('Bingo') Johnson, came into the terminal, walked over to me and said, "Congratulations!"

I was completely nonplussed and asked why he had said that. "After you had left the meeting this morning, the council decided to appoint you to the post of county sanitary inspector."

I was unable to speak or think. Here was I, on my way to the funeral of my boss for the past fifteen years, and I had been given his job without even having to apply for it! I could not even feel any elation, even though it was the aim which I had been pursuing since I was appointed apprentice in 1949. In actual fact, it did me no favours in the eyes of other deputes and qualified assistants in Scotland as there was only a certain number of county sanitary inspector posts available and these were normally hotly contended. No one else had, in this instance, been given the opportunity even to apply which was, to say the least, a bit unusual.

However, in the interim, I was on my way to the funeral which I duly attended and met some of Mr Hastings' many friends and relations. Several of those attending were county sanitary inspectors for other areas and they maintained a friendship with me and supported me throughout the remainder of their respective working lives. This was the first funeral I had ever attended where there were women present and where the mourners retired to a hostelry after the committal proceedings. Not like the Lerwick of the 1960s.

During the past few months, both the qualified assistant and milk officer had resigned and moved away. So here was I, at last head of department with the responsibility of ensuring compliance with the mountain of legislation which was within the remit of the County Sanitary Department of Zetland County Council. The only problem was that I had no staff other than my secretary, Chris Smith, to whom I can never express sufficient thanks for always remaining cool, calm and very collected through the occasional traumatic moments which followed. I had for a long time harboured the hope that the filing system and office organisation in the department could be made more closely related to the changes in legislation which had been happening over the years, but this would take time and the first priority was to appoint a qualified assistant. Adverts were placed in all the regular papers in Scotland to no avail as the salary being offered in Shetland was not conducive to anyone having to move here from an established post on the mainland. The salaries in England were even higher than in Scotland, but I persuaded the finance department to have one attempt at producing an applicant from south of the border with little hope of producing the result which followed.

I actually received a telephone call at home from a man speaking from Liverpool who had been told of my advert by a relative who had read it in *The Shetland Times*. This was a qualified sanitary inspector with several years experience, including meat inspection; he had been on holiday in Shetland several times and, being under the threat of redundancy from his present post, he was very keen to apply for the job in my department. This was Alan C. Blackburn, who was interviewed and offered the post, which he accepted and duly arrived here with his wife and young family in September 1964, at the start of a partnership which lasted until he retired, and a friendship which lasted until his death in 2005. Alan was the absolutely ideal person for the job. His grandparents were both from Shetland, he had relatives in Dunrossness and, in some ways most important of all, he had been a merchant seaman, a prisoner of war in Germany where he had been in the company of other Shetlanders, and later master-mariner.

When one is visiting a household in Shetland, say regarding an improvement grant and, in order to achieve the best possible outcome it is patently obvious that, for instance, the best room, the holy of holies, will have to become the kitchen, and the front door blocked-up, it is always preferable, if not essential, to have some prepared preamble to break the news more gradually. This can take the form of a discussion on the news of the fishing, the weather, the price of lambs and so on, but Alan had the added benefit of his life in the merchant navy to draw upon. In those days there was, more often than not, a photo or painting of a merchant ship on some wall in a house. Alan, again more often than not, would have some knowledge of the ship or the shipping line or the port where the ship had been pictured, and this was a magic way of gaining the friendship and confidence of the householder and they more readily accepted that what we were proposing was in fact good sense.

The middle part of the 1960s was a very low point in the history of modern Shetland. The basic industries on which the prosperity of the islands must depend, fishing and knitwear, were both at a very low ebb and many young people were emigrating in order to find employment. The only place in Shetland with any prospect of employment was Lerwick, and the number of applicants for houses there grew accordingly, raising the spectre of depopulation in the more remote parts of Shetland. The County Council decided to attempt to stem the flow to the town and central area of Shetland by establishing 'holding points' in the North, South and West Mainland, the districts chosen being Brae, Sandwick and Aith. Council houses would be built there and nowhere else, and businesses looking for sites would be encouraged to go there also. While this obviously did not stop the movement towards Lerwick, it certainly made a big difference and these three districts grew in importance as a consequence.

CHAPTER ELEVEN

Up-Helly-A'

FROM a ridiculously early age I was indoctrinated into the mysteries, tradition and rituals of – no, not the masons – but Up-Helly-A', by my mother who, although both her parents were non-Shetlanders who had incidentally arrived via the south entrance of Lerwick harbour, was one of the most fervent supporters of the festival I have ever encountered, and I have encountered a few. She came from the generation when there were no halls and the guizers went around various houses in Lerwick, one of which was 54 Burgh Road where the Campbell family lived at that time. Her brother, John Campbell, was guizer jarl in 1923 and I suspect that there was a fair bit of excitement around at the time! In 1904 my father was also in what was, according to Erling Clausen, the earliest squad ever photographed, and he was a contemporary and great friend of J.W. Robertson who was the first jarl in 1906 so I have a bit of 'pedigree' I suppose.

Anyway, from about the time that I could stand, my mother would dress me in a very primitive cloak, with a helmet, shield and axe made from cardboard and silver paper. As the years passed, things became a bit more sophisticated and the coopers at the Anglo-Scottish made a galley on wheels for me, and my pals would join in the burning. I have no recollection of where this took place or whether there were any torches involved, but no doubt a good time was had by all.

For as long as I had lived in the house, the basement of 55 King Harald Street had always been used as a squad room. Brother Jim was in many different squads and, as traditionalists might expect, I was banned from the premises until the festival was over, in case I revealed anything about the suit or act.

Up-Helly-A' 1936, with Ian MacKay, son of postmaster.

Anglo-Scottish Herring Co., Browns Road, Lerwick, where my galleys were built.

As I mentioned earlier, on Up-Helly-A' night 1939, there was a breathtaking display of aurora borealis. I can remember standing on the top step at '55' and the whole sky was glowing red from north to south. This, of course, was the last festival until after the war and it took until 1949 before the old order returned, with a jarl and procession. At this time I was still in the RAF so it was not until 1950 that I was able to join a squad. That year we appeared as the 'Happy Heppies', actually an advert for Hepworths who provided made-to-measure suits for us, dressed as elves. I must admit that this was a rather smarter outfit than what became the norm thereafter, white boiler suits, dyed, then bleached, then painted and so on!

As an aside, I have memories of a bonfire at the Waarie Geo which I thought might have been the first attempt at a fire festival of some kind. However, prompted by a conversation with Ian Fraser, a bit of research at the Shetland Archives into *The Shetland Times* of 9th November, 1945, revealed that this was in fact part of 'Thanksgiving Week', another fund-raising effort. During the day there had been a parade which included a march-past by the remaining military units in Shetland and the youth organisations, music being provided by the British Legion Pipe Band and the Boys' Brigade Flute and Drum Band.

A nine-foot long galley, named 'Sejr' or 'Victory', had been built by the 'dock's boys' and torches had also been made. In the evening there was a procession, in good weather, from the Hillhead to King Harald Street where there was a turning movement. From there the procession moved on to the Waarie Geo where the torches were thrown on to a huge bonfire and the assembled crowd sang 'Song of Liberty' to the music of Elgar played by the BB Band. I am almost certain that we, the pupils at the Institute, had been taught the words of the song by teacher Bill Rhind, an accomplished singer, in order to prepare for this event, as some of the words still come to mind ... "*All men must be free*".

On this occasion the galley was not put to the torch but was kept, at the suggestion of Mr J.G. Peterson, to be used at the appropriate time for a 'miniature Up-Helly-A". A further report in *The Shetland Times* of 1st February, 1946, shows that on the last Tuesday of January, the galley 'Sejr', with guizer jarl Ian Fraser, was taken in procession through the streets on a night of dreadful weather to the Waarie Geo where, in the time-honoured manner, the jarl descended and the torches were hurled into the galley. The traditional Up-Helly-A' songs were sung to music from two cornets and one trombone. This was the first time that a unified junior Up-Helly-A' had taken place, the previous tradition being several, much smaller, individual processions and galleys.

I normally pride myself that I have a fairly good retentive memory but for some obscure reason I have no recollection of any of the foregoing (sorry Ian!) apart from the singing at the bonfire when, in any event, I would have been in the Boys' Brigade Band – all very puzzling.

For the next three years I was at college in Edinburgh so did not rejoin the squad until 1954, and from then I was a regular member and the basement reverted to its former winter use – very handy for me.

In 1957 I was appointed to the Up-Helly-A' committee. I really had no idea of what this entailed and had I but known I might have thought twice before accepting. I was under the impression that the committee consisted of men who either built the galley or made the torches and both of these pursuits are well outside my capabilities. I was, therefore, somewhat surprised to be stopped on the street by ex-jarl G. W. Blance (Dodie Willie) and questioned as to why I had not been at a meeting of the 'jokes committee'. Accustomed to council procedure, I responded that I had not been elected to that committee, to which his answer was, "You were put on the jokes committee to write jokes, AND YOU _WILL_ WRITE JOKES!" One did not argue with Dodie Willie, so from then on I wrote jokes and many of them did, over the years, appear on the bill or collecting sheet.

There was tremendous camaraderie at the jokes committee but the problem was that, if the jokes were written too early in the year, everyone had forgotten the reason by the end of January. Many were the evenings when, together with Alan Anderson, Jack Scott and others, I was helpless with laughter at something which had suddenly come to mind but, when written down, was certainly not for publication or, when reconsidered in the cold light of day, was not in the least amusing! The perpetual problem is that a certain

111

number of words are needed to provide adequate text for the proclamation. As many as possible of these should either be amusing, or *double entendres,* or preferably both. The *double entendres* are always shown in red, so as many as possible give the bill a more colourful appearance. The final jokes committee is normally filled with a sense of foreboding, too few words, not funny enough, no defacer, can we really say that? And then the final panic when the bill is being painted – I was once handed a bit of paper about eight o'clock on the Monday evening before Up-Helly-A' day and told, "We're short of 50 words – write." It was strange if something had not happened worthy of note during the last few hours and that always makes the whole content more up-to-date, so I usually succeeded.

In the early days the jokes committee met in a building in Fort Road, now demolished. Meetings began about 9.30pm and lasted as long as the more senior members felt necessary. These senior ex-jarls – Tom Henry, John Peter Smith, Bruce Laurenson and Dodie Willie – were seemingly indefatigable and, when they had exhausted all their expertise and that of the other members in joke making, they would thereafter repair to one or other of their houses and continue there. The junior member was always expected to accompany them, but I began to rebel at a very early stage. It became very obvious that the capacity to make usable material very quickly waned as the evening progressed and most of the time thereafter was spent in idle chatter. Meg was sitting at home at Baila with two infants, not too enamoured with the situation. I therefore made myself somewhat unpopular on both sides by stating quite firmly that I was leaving the meetings in time to be home at midnight – no doubt earning a 'Cinderella' reputation in the process. Nevertheless, I persisted in this until I finally stopped attending, not so many years ago.

Having joined the Up-Helly-A' committee in 1957 I should not have been jarl until after the normal 16 years, in 1973, but because of various reasons, several members of the committee departed before their turn came and I became jarl in 1967. This coincided with the return of our family from 7 Baila to 55 King Harald Street, of which I shall write more later. During the 'flittin' I was transporting boxes of books in our Ford Anglia, which had a high lip on the boot, and at some stage in the proceedings I must have overdone things as I found myself unable to move, my back was in agony, and I had to ask someone to release the brake on the car before I could drive home. I crawled upstairs to bed and there I remained for the next couple of weeks. When Dennis Coutts came to take the photo to use on the cover of the 1967 Up-Helly-A' programme I had to be rolled out of bed and perched in an Orkney chair. Purists will note that this is the only photo where the jarl is not wearing the coat of mail – it was far too heavy! I had a black t-shirt over my pyjamas and Norman Baker, one of my squad, was kneeling at one side holding the shield and either Gordon or Richard was at the other side supporting the axe – some 'Hardy Viking'! I was taken to the Gilbert Bain Hospital and given manipulation in the theatre, with some of the staff marching round me singing the Up-Helly-A' songs. Thanks to the ministrations of Meg, Dr Neil Cadenhead and Surgeon Ronnie Cumming (two of the three, keen guizers), I was eventually able to get on my feet again in time to fulfil my duty as guizer jarl, representing Erling Skakki, albeit wearing a big leather and steel brace to keep me in one piece!

It was a great relief to be able to complete my time on the Up-Helly-A' committee in the appropriate manner, especially when I was able to be accompanied by Gordon (12) and Richard (10), and we even have a photo which includes Jill (7), when we called at Bells Brae School. A particularly special moment came when the galley, with me and the boys onboard, stopped during the turning movement in front of 55 King Harald Street where Meg and Jill were watching from the terrace and my mother, by now too frail to participate, was sitting in the upstairs window with a grandstand view. It was an unforgettable experience, soaked as I was in the downpour, even after stepping down out of the galley to become just another ex-jarl.

In those days a very important visit, months prior to the event, was to the 'oracle', at that time ex-jarl and brilliant artist Tom Henry, who was well versed in the sagas. It was after consulting him that I had decided to represent the Norse jarl, Erling Skakki, and Tom was very keen that I should include bows and arrows in the armaments for the squad. On the other hand, having seen the antics of some other squads as the long evenings progressed, I was rather reluctant, visualising the A &E department at the Gilbert Bain Hospital being

Jarl Erling Skakki with sons Gordon and Richard, 1967.

filled with patients suffering from arrow wounds – not the kind of body piercing popular today. We settled on axes, shields and spears, the latter being a bit *avant garde* at the time. I have to admit that our outfits were in no way as sophisticated as those of today, but I am also sure that we had as much enjoyment and pleasure at approximately £60 per person as is evident today at considerably more. One more year on the committee and, in 1968, I was Chief Marshall in charge of the procession which, I am glad to say, went off without a hitch. This was the end of my involvement with the Up-Helly-A' committee but not with Up-Helly-A'.

As I said earlier, my mother was of the generation where the squads visited private houses but as the years passed the size of the festival grew and halls were opened for the entertainment of guizers and guests. My mother was among the first of the ladies who became hostesses, in her case at the Grand Hotel, and she continued in that role until 1966 when Meg and I were asked to take over her share. After I left the committee I returned to being a squad member but, after a year, Dodie Willie, the most senior of the male hosts at the Grand, said that I had to make up my mind as to whether I was going to be a guizer or a host, as the hall was short of male hosts to man the doors etc. The great majority of the work involved in being a host/hostess at a hall falls on the ladies who have to prepare sandwiches and other consumables for the starving mass of guizers who descend upon the supper tables. Meg had, of course, been landed with this whilst I gallivanted with the squad. I decide that it was time to show a modicum of responsibility and chose to give up the squad membership, although guizing is a wonderful way of having a great night out. And I do mean 'guizing', when one is suitably camouflaged and anonymous until at least the end of the first dance, unlike today when most guizers do not even wear any kind of mask.

I think that my favourite night was when I represented Mortimer Manson when he was in charge of a drive to collect money for the restoration of the Böd of Gremista. A perfect mask of Mortimer had been made by Bunty Hunter and I borrowed a hat and coat which were exactly the type he used. The squad was called 'Böddy can you spare a dime?' and we had a model of the Böd in which I was concealed. At an appropriate moment the roof opened and I appeared. This was especially fitting at the Queens Hotel where Mortimer was sitting taking notes for the *Shetland News* and we had our photo taken together – happy days!

One other strange coincidence happened when I was on duty in the corridor at the Grand Hotel. The hosts had to check that no uninvited people gained entrance and I spotted a man dressed in 'civvies' among the squad members so asked him if he I actually belonged to the squad. He said that he was the bus driver, and produced his pass to confirm. For some reason I was curious and engaged him in conversation. Believe it or not, this was Paddy Byrne, the Irishman with whom I had shared a sailing yacht at Kasfareet on the Suez Canal in 1948, nineteen years earlier. Paddy was working at the fish processing factory at Brown's Road, and we were able to meet occasionally before he once again disappeared.

Meg and I were hosts at the Grand Hotel for fifteen years and then, when the function room became 'Posers' nightclub, the hosts and hostesses moved to Clickimin Games Hall and we retired. While Meg stopped attending from then, I continued to be invited as an ex-host and was able to enjoy watching the various squads performing their acts, and meet old friends and fellow guizers. My final connection with the hall was in 2006 when our grandson, Robert, became junior guizer jarl, again representing Erling Skakki, to my great delight.

Junior jarl Robert Smith and grandad – 'Erling Skakkis', 2006 and 1967.

One very unexpected holiday across the globe took place in 1978 when two ex-jarls found themselves in Japan. The story begins a long way back when there was an exchange of children's artwork between Lerwick and a school outside Tokyo. Through this exchange, teacher and ex-jarl Tommy Moncrieff was befriended by the artist, an Englishman resident in Japan who had organised the event and he, in turn, had been telling his friends in Japan about Up-Helly-A'. To cut a long story short, in 1975, completely unannounced, a Japanese gentleman arrived in Lerwick on the Saturday before Up-Helly-A' asking for Tom Moncrieff. Tommy was teaching so he asked me if I would take the man with me during the day when I was doing my visits in the county area, and this is how I first met Shinjiro Izumi. He was just here for a few days but seemed, like others, to fall in love with the place, even in mid-winter. Anyway, he returned twice in succeeding years, once with his wife. In 1978, again out of the blue and with no prior consultation, a letter arrived inviting Tom and I (no wives) to visit him in his home in Japan for two weeks in August. Enclosed were tickets for the return flight with Aeroflot from London to Tokyo and cheques to cover our expenses while away from home. We discovered that he was, in fact, a very important businessman, having twice won the trophy for the best inventor of the year in Japan, so this was his way of repaying our meagre hospitality while he was in Shetland. The outcome would fill another volume, but suffice to say that we had a wonderful holiday and travelled widely in that remarkable country. Izumi died in a car accident some years ago but his wife and I still exchange Christmas cards.

Despite it getting a lot of criticism, I still am of the opinion that Up-Helly-A' is a wonderful festival bringing together people from all walks of life as 'guizers', whether they are unemployed, doctors, apprentices or, for that matter, the Lord Lieutenant. It is a great 'leveller', self-policed, and woe-betide any squad which steps out of line. Without the ladies behind the scenes there would be no festival as we know it and the amount of work which the hostesses devote cannot be overestimated. Without the ladies in the hall, with whom would the guizers dance? One criticism which I have is that these days, all too often, the squad members seem to leave the hall as soon as they have finished their act. They should at least stay for the first dance which, after all, is their choice. In my opinion, the number of participants is now at a stage where it really cannot expand further without several additional venues being available during the evening. The idea that the festival is performed as a tourist attraction is nonsense. It is first and foremost a Lerwick festival, primarily for the enjoyment of the guizers and their friends, the culmination of countless hours of work and companionship (for the males at least) over the winter months, with any spare invitations or tickets being available to other local supporters. It is, in my opinion, completely unfair for visitors to pay the exorbitant fare to come to Shetland (at least until a venue is found for those attracted here by the tourist industry) and find that, after the procession – which incidentally takes only about 45 minutes – they are left to wander aimlessly around the deserted town – this is not the true spirit of Up-Helly-A'… I'm just a traditionalist ex-jarl, get me out of here!

CHAPTER TWELVE

Back to home life

THINGS were changing so far as the family was concerned. As I mentioned earlier, my father had to leave Peterhead and return home in 1957. Although his general health and his mind were remarkably good despite his age, he was gradually becoming more stiff and housebound but when he took to his bed there was no thought that this was anything serious. However, within a very short time, his whole system started to break down and he died on 17th August, 1964. My mother was still relatively fit and well able to look

Dad and Mum at 7 Baila, 1960s.

7 Baila now.

after herself, and we were often at '55' with the family who loved her stories and piano playing. Gordon, in particular, seemed to have an exceptional memory and one of our early memories is of him reciting, word perfect, the story of the old woman who was going to market to buy a pig, *"But piggie would not jump over the stile and she could not get home that night"* – I haven't tried him recently but I bet he can still remember it.

At Baila our neighbours were Alec and Kitty Gray and their daughter Anne. Anne was a leading light in the Lifeboys and both Gordon and Richard joined and were members, if perhaps not the keenest in the pack. As happens, sport again supervened and their membership did not last as long in the Boys' Brigade as did my own, but by then there were many other attractions. Jill, when her time came, was actually a keen member of the Brownies.

As time passed my mother was becoming progressively less able to look after the very awkward accommodation at '55' and we decided to move back in to town to be with her and share the house as best we could. This was just before Christmas 1967, and this was the 'flittin' where I wrecked my back, so

I was not a great deal of help for some time thereafter! We re-arranged the way the rooms had been organised so that the boys and Jill occupied the two rooms on the top floor. On the first floor my mother had her bedroom and a sitting room, together with our bedroom and the shared bathroom, and on the ground floor we had our sitting room, kitchen and scullery. Meals were always taken together and one of the boys would normally go up to 'Gaga's' room to escort her safely down the stairs. (She insisted on being called 'Gaga', although she was perhaps one of the cleverest women of her time.)

As I have said, I was delighted that she was able to sit in the window of her sitting room and watch me as guizer jarl in the crowning moments of my years of association with the festival. After this she gradually began to fail and was latterly hospitalised, passing away on the 8th May, 1967. She had enjoyed a varied life, and I shall only attempt to give a few examples of her many public-spirited involvements. She was a founder member of the Shetland Branch of the Order of the Eastern Star, she was awarded the Silver Badge of the Royal National Lifeboat Institution, she was Patron of the Shetland Fiddlers' Society, Chairwoman of the Zetland Education Authority, a Volunteer Nursing Auxiliary during World War Two, and still able, to the original surprise of the Director of Education John H. Spence, regularly to complete the 'Ximines' crossword in the *Observer*.

So, we now had '55' to ourselves, and the family began to enjoy the more accessible enjoyments of the swings in the play park, the putting green in the flower park, and football at the 'pubbie' (the 'public' or Gilbertson Park). I can remember standing on the steps at '55' blowing a whistle to call the boys in from a game in the play park and them returning with their ball to the chagrin of the other participants, and also in the almost dark of a fine summer evening shouting into the public park, where I could hear voices but see nobody, that it was time for home, if not bed.

The proximity to St Clements Hall was also a great attraction and the prowess of each of our family in badminton is in many ways thanks to that edifice and the kindness and patience of the senior players who helped and coached the young ones.

At the office by 1967-68, things had begun to change in a most dramatic way. The fishing and knitwear industries bloomed to such an extent that houses had to be provided for incoming workers to operate the fish processing factories and knitwear machines. A cargo boat actually went from Lerwick to the factory in Norway where the wooden 'Fjogstad' houses were fabricated, and carried them back to be unloaded as near as possible to where they were to be erected. This saved possible damage and loss of components had they been shipped from elsewhere. The assessment of applicants and the allocation of houses was becoming a more and more important sideline of the department and, within another couple of years, the flow of applicants turned into a torrent when North Sea Oil was discovered.

Not all that long afterwards I was lucky enough to be able to appoint a qualified assistant, Dave Okill, by coincidence again from Liverpool. A keen ornithologist in his spare time, Dave never missed the opportunity to visit remote corners like Fair Isle for the purpose of water samples or house inspections or whatever.

Finally I was able to obtain the services of a milk and food hygiene officer, Jim Barr. Jim had been born and brought up in the farming area of Ayrshire and was a loyal and dedicated worker. This then was my staff and, apart from changes in the secretarial personnel, they remained with me during the rest of my working life, with Alan retiring a few years before I did.

A regular job was visiting food premises to condemn food, especially tins which were 'blown' or had passed their sell-by date, when a certificate was issued to the shopkeeper which he could use to claim replacements. On one occasion however the consignment was somewhat larger than usual. This was during a shipping strike when the normal supplies of food had not arrived for some time and the Scottish Office in Edinburgh decided, in their wisdom, to send a landing craft loaded with goods which were standing in the warehouse at Aberdeen. Weather conditions were not good and the blunt-nosed craft had to make for shelter in Peterhead before continuing to Lerwick. Berthed at Victoria Pier after several days rather than hours, this vessel was an object of considerable curiosity for the local ship-watchers and a steady stream of folk were walking up the gangway to have a look. Having been told about the conditions on board by an 'innocent bystander' I went down in my official capacity to examine the cargo but was refused permission to board as the ship was part of the armed forces and not open to Local Government officials! I therefore walked back up the pier, back down again, straight up the gangway *incognito* and looked into the hold. The hold was, of course, uncovered and on the way north, sea water had been constantly splashing over the bow ramp so that the cargo was lying in several feet of water. The cargo consisted of bags of flour, vegetables, meat carcases wrapped in canvas, and many other items intended for the local wholesalers and shops. Also in the hold was a tractor, out of which a considerable amount of oil had floated. The entire cargo was contaminated in some manner, so the whole lot was conveyed to the dump and, mercifully, normal shipping services resumed soon after.

During the summer I used to go fishing for olicks off Sumburgh Head with Meg's father in his boat, appropriately named *The Five Sisters*, and had many fine fresh-fish suppers when we landed our catch at Grutness pier, just a few yards from the house. I also, for a short time, tried trout fishing without any great success. The best days I had were with a couple of friends when we drove to the top of Collafirth Hill in Northmavine then spent the whole day walking round and fishing the lochs on Ronas Hill. The lochs seemed to be full of reasonably sized fish and it was a really rewarding experience.

One beautiful Shetland summer day I actually took Gordon and Richard with me and carried a rucksack with all the necessary gear to cook a fish should we be lucky enough to be successful. (In those days, before the 'oilies'

Richard and Gordon, Ronas Hill.

arrived on the hill with helicopters and fished out the lochs, it would have been a miracle had we not caught at least one fish.) In due course we landed enough for our meal, the stove was assembled, the fish gutted and the oatmeal applied, and the frying-pan put to use. The fish were eaten off flat stones with our hands, washed before and afterwards in the loch, and a great day was had by all with photos as proof – how I now wish we had done it more often.

I think that it must have been about this time that the five-day-working-week was instituted for Zetland County Council amid cries of "How will we get all the work done?" from some dedicated oldies. However, we managed somehow, and having the whole weekend off allowed us to think about maybe buying or renting a cottage somewhere in the country, to "get away from it all". This is not as easy as it sounds in a small place like Shetland, where ones movements are almost public knowledge. For example, if we were on holiday or even on an outing, it was not uncommon for me to be approached by someone who had learned that we were in the area, wanting advice on their drainage system or something similar and it was difficult to refuse without being rude.

We looked around in the North and West Mainland, as we were assured of a welcome at Grutness whenever we cared to call there, and eventually learned of a vacant croft house at Afrigarth, near Bridge of Walls. We approached the tenant of the croft who lived elsewhere and he was willing for us to use the property provided that we kept it wind and watertight to the best of our ability. The house had most recently been used as a club room for a group of young people in the area but was now unused. It consisted of the usual but, ben and closet on the ground floor, and two very low-ceilinged attic rooms. In addition there was a barn at one end and, accessible by a door through the gable wall of the ben end, there was a large room which had been used as the club room and this also had an outside door.

The property was still connected to the electricity mains but there was no piped water and no drainage facilities, all adding to the sense of adventure. There was a burn at the side and the boys constructed a dam with an overflow pipe which served as the source of all water during our occupancy. There was a 'small room' outside at the back of the house and there we installed an 'Elsan' chemical toilet. There was a 'Victoress' stove, a table and a few chairs remaining in the house, and we gathered such other essential items as were needed to make the place at least partly habitable.

The roof was the traditional tarred felt and this was thoroughly re-coated every year we were in occupation. The stone walls were whitewashed with the ingoes of the windows painted black for effect. The internal walls were wood lined so some were painted and others 'decorated' with pages from wallpaper books.

There were several dilapidated houses in the Walls area where the thatched roofs had fallen in and I approached the owner of one to see what his intentions were. "I'm going to burn it out and make a store," was the answer.

I asked if we could have a look to see if there was any usable stuff left inside, as was often the case when a house was vacated. "The door is jammed but go in through the roof and take anything you find, but if there is a box of sovereigns – that's mine!" he said.

Afrigarth, 1970s.

So, we all had a search and found various 'treasures' which fitted very well into the Afrigarth scene, including a chair, and a restin' chair which was affected with woodworm but sat outside and served as a garden seat for many years. We made benches for seats and spare beds, Meg sewing covers for the foam rubber cushions, making curtains and so on (or sew on). No phone or television of course, the nearest public 'phone being at the very useful Bridge of Walls shop with Jack Tulloch as the purveyor of every kind of goods and chattels imaginable.

By this time I had bought a 12-foot fibreglass dinghy with an outboard motor and it was put to good use in the voes in the neighbourhood. One evening a local came to visit and suggested that my boat would be ideal from which to set a trout net. This expedition had to take place after dark, this being late August, so we had to set off about 11pm, dressed in black and wearing balaclavas, with muffled oars – just joking of course! The net was duly set, but because the Walls Show was next day the police were expected in the area in the very early morning so the net had to be lifted before 5am. There was a furtive knock on the window at Afrigarth, I reluctantly rose and we set off again. When we approached the net in the gloom we could see several white objects caught in the meshes and we had visions of a great success, but as we drew nearer we realised to our disgust that the white objects were actually plastic bottles, and that was our entire catch.

We had hoped to be able to buy the house at Afrigarth from the tenant crofter, and he was willing to sell it if he could get it decrofted, but in the interim Miss Foster, the owner of the Vaila estate on which the croft stood, died. The estate was entailed and we were advised that a long time could elapse before any transactions could take place.

Gradually the lure of the town, football, Islesburgh Youth Club and other youthful enterprises began to overcome the desire for the country life, so reluctantly Meg and I packed up our gear and moved back to 'base camp' at '55'.

CHAPTER THIRTEEN

North Sea Oil

IN the beginning of the 1970s strange vessels began to appear in Shetland waters, but this time they were not Russians but American registered supply boats, like the *Caribe Tide*, a long, low craft with a high bow and bridge and a low afterdeck for cargo. When one looks at the huge supply boats of today it seems incredible that these early 'midgets' were able to stand the rigours of the North Sea – but they did. As county sanitary inspector I obviously had a role to play in the protection of the environment from this unexpected and unknown, so far as I was concerned, threat to our livelihoods and way of life.

My first involvement was at the spur of Victoria Pier where a company involved in supplying drilling mud – barytes – had erected silos for transferring the barytes to the supply boats. This product was very dusty, and when uncovered boxes of fish were being loaded on to the north boats at Victoria Pier they were being contaminated with the dust being discharged from the vents during operations. I wrote to the company and insisted that the silos should be ventilated below the surface of the water instead of into the open air, to be met with the response: "We have always done it like this."

I was forced to reply that they were not going to do it like that any more, in Lerwick at any rate, and eventually the problem was resolved. Later, of course, the whole operation was transferred to the huge 'all purpose' base called Norscot, built by the Fred Olsen organisation at the Green Head.

The oil industry had obviously decided that they were going to have to provide a facility in Shetland where the offshore oil could be stabilised by removing excess gas and water before being shipped further for refining. However, Shetland was already in a strong position so far as employment was concerned so, in a way, they needed us more than we needed them, which put our negotiators in a somewhat advantageous bargaining position.

Somewhere in the region of 30 different oil companies each wanted to have their own treatment facility in Shetland which was totally unacceptable to the local authority, who decreed that one 'joint-user' facility would be permitted. A senior member of BP Shipping, Captain Tom Copeman, came to Shetland to assess the different voes and anchorages which might be suitable for such a terminal and the final choice fell on Sullom Voe. The terminal itself would be built on Calback Ness. This site was remote, had deep water close to the shore, and little or no environmental implications such as loss of habitat or unique plant life. Furthermore, most of the buildings in the area were the ruins of the World War Two RAF Coastal Command station, so any modern development might even be, in some instances, an improvement.

The different oil companies were not in the least bit impressed with the idea of working together with one another. "This has never been done before," was once again the cry. But when faced with the fact that "This is how it is going to be," common sense prevailed and the Sullom Voe Association (SVA) was formed, incorporating members from all the participating oil companies and representatives from Zetland County Council.

All sorts of ramifications and shenanigans were going on with various entrepreneurs trying to collar the best sites and anyone wishing to read more about this can do so elsewhere. Suffice to say that, through the Zetland County Council Act 1974, this small local authority gained a huge reputation and a huge bank balance through the wisdom and doggedness of a very few wise men of the time. Outstanding amongst these were the convener, George W. Blance (ex-headmaster and ex-jarl) and chief executive Ian R. Clark (formerly director of finance).

My own involvement began with huge batches of virtually incomprehensible plans being submitted for planning approval. Kindly consider that until very recently I had considered oil as being something to put into the car occasionally, and here I was confronted with plans for a series of fractionisation trains, clean and oily water drains (which were a bit more in my line), and ballast water treatment systems. The oil industry had, of course, world class experts in all the required categories and legal eagles to query any qualification which might be placed on their proposals by the local authority. At this point I will, however, put on record my appreciation of the immense amount of work, personal time and dedication, which successive industry environmental representatives devoted to the task of preserving, so far as was practically possible, the existing state of the Shetland environment and, in fact, on occasion improving it.

There was still no separate planning department but the council now, very wisely, decided that staff should be recruited. The first head of department was Mike Fenwick, but before he arrived to take up post two young ladies, Jean Spence and Janet Askew, held the fort and began the task of cataloguing the mass of paperwork which began to flow in ever increasing volumes.

The original plans were submitted by Shell, but several amendments and major alterations were required and eventually a new submission was made by BP, who became terminal managers on behalf of the other participants. There were, in particular, two items which caused much grief. Firstly, the insistence by the local authority that, if practicable, the giant crude-oil storage caverns should be underground, while the oil industry wanted to construct tanks on the surface. A mining firm ('Geostock', I think) came to Shetland and drilled a tunnel deep under Calback Ness to assess the suitability of the rock. It was found to be too friable and fragmented so that, even if 'caverns' were excavated underground they would thereafter have to be lined with concrete to make them watertight and this would entail a huge additional cost and considerable delay to the project.

Consideration then took place on the proposal to erect the huge surface tanks which one sees today. The original plans had these tanks without individual 'bunds' to retain any oil which might be spilled or lost through an accident. The council insisted on individual watertight bunds for each tank – I think the capacity to be 110 per cent of the content of each tank – to allow for possible water content in the bund from rainfall.

The second *contretemps* was also in relation to these tanks, when the county weights and measures inspector, Stanley Henry, who was also in charge of petroleum spirit licensing legislation, refused to approve the design of the tanks unless they were provided with an extra reinforced steel beam round each tank near the top to prevent potential damage from the extreme winds experienced in Shetland. In time this was eventually agreed and work on the site gathered momentum.

Visits to the construction site were carefully controlled and one was, in the early days, taken in a company vehicle across the beach at the end of Garths Voe, there being no road. On the site itself there was apparent mayhem but this was presumably controlled as well. Huge dumpers and earth movers were charging around at breakneck speeds, driven by devil-may-care 'wannabe Stirling Moss' youths wearing t-shirts and bandanas. Vast quantities of heather, earth and peat were removed and dumped into Orka Voe and in due course rumours began to circulate that bulldozers and the like had vanished into the morass! Soon a new road was built from Firth to the terminal and the road from Brae was greatly improved.

To accommodate the first 1,200 workers, the council erected a construction village at the top of the hill at Firth. Because of the possibility of hundreds of bored workers descending on the local villages and Lerwick, it was decided that this place should have every reasonable leisure facility, including a huge theatre, reading and television rooms, betting shop, canteen, 'welly bar', medical centre, a place for worship and so on. The men were working 12-hour shifts so actually were ready for a bit of relaxation when they finished and I can remember only one day when there was an 'invasion' of Lerwick. This was during a strike at the terminal and buses transported many workers to the town. However, it was a beautiful, sunny summer's day and they sat on the wall below the post office and wandered along the street and piers before returning north again, and I am almost certain that no problems whatsoever resulted from this incursion. The food produced in the canteen was really of hotel standard and the portions served were mind-boggling.

While on the subject of food, the supply of this commodity to the offshore installations was a vital part of the daily organisation of the oil industry. On one occasion a supply boat had left Aberdeen on Boxing Day for a rig to the east of Shetland, but because of weather conditions it had been unable to deliver its cargo, which was in an unrefrigerated container on deck.

By the time the vessel reached Lerwick it had been at sea for almost a week and I was asked to examine the cargo and issue certificates for the food which was no longer fit for human consumption. Together with Alan Blackburn, always of inestimable help as a former seaman and master-mariner, I went on board and found the ship virtually deserted. The only member of the crew to be found was the mate, the others having gone 'up town' to celebrate the New Year.

When the mate opened the container it was rather like a gruesome Aladdin's cave, with defrosted bovine livers in plastic bags, sides of bacon, workers' boots, brake linings, electric bulbs, ropes, boiler suits and what appeared to be enough defrosted sausages to feed the entire population of Shetland. The whole lot was obviously for the dump, but just in case there was any idea of any of the foodstuffs being 'offered' to the local shops, Alan and I sprayed all the food with disinfectant and dye. As lunch time approached we told the mate to close and lock the container and then left the ship. Returning after lunch we were rather startled to see scories flying across the harbour with strings of sausages in their beaks and, on closer inspection, most of the gull population of Lerwick inside the container. Obviously the mate had decided to join his compatriots before locking the door! We then withdrew and told the vessel's agents that the problem was out of our hands.

As the workforce at Sullom Voe gradually increased, the oil industry constructed three separate units, each accommodating 600 workers, at the Toft construction village, with all the same facilities as at Firth. In due course even this was not enough and two ships were chartered and moored in Garths Voe to house mainly supervisory and administrative staff. These ships were the *Stena Baltica* and the *Rangatira*, a former ferry on the route between North and South Islands, New Zealand.

Apart from feeding the workers in their accommodation there was also a need for canteens on site and ten canteens capable of serving 100 men, and one capable of serving 200 men, were erected within the terminal area. These were all supplied from a central kitchen, the food being transported across the site in heated containers. All these catering facilities were within the remit of my department in terms of the food hygiene regulations and regular visits were carried out, which incidentally gave one the opportunity to sample the varied menus on offer! It is due to the capability and to the credit of the catering staff in all these very varied premises that not one case of food poisoning was reported to my department or the on-site medical unit during the whole of my association with the terminal, a truly remarkable record in my opinion considering that there were approximately 6,000 people being regularly fed.

Protection of the environment from the seemingly innumerable sources of potential pollution or physical damage during the construction and operation of this massive facility was also paramount. To this end, in 1974, a group of experts from universities and other independent bodies involved in environmental protection were called together by BP, and the body called the Sullom Voe Environmental Advisory Group (SVEAG) was formed. The remit was to establish a monitoring strategy which would take into account the various potential sources of pollution and provide recommendations as to the best practicable means of preventing or controlling potential adverse effects. In due course, however, there was seen to be a possible conflict of interest in that the chairmanship was in the hands of BP, so that body was disbanded and, like the phoenix, it rose again in the form of the Shetland Oil Terminal Environmental Advisory Group (SOTEAG).

The chairman of SOTEAG was Professor George Dunnet, of Aberdeen University, and the group consisted of experts from all the various fields associated with the environment. Local input came from the likes of Geordie Hunter and later John Goodlad of the Shetland Fishermen's Association, Bobby Tulloch of the Royal Society for the Protection of Birds (and much else), Shetland Bird Club, Shetland Farmers' Association and, from Shetland Islands Council, there were the director of planning, Mike Fenwick, and myself as director of environmental health. Speaking for myself, these experts could have me baffled with science within a couple of sentences, but they were always polite enough (or almost always) to explain patiently the situation as they saw it from their scientific viewpoint. Quite often it was an injection of 'midder wit' from one of the 'locals' which produced a solution to a seemingly insurmountable scientific impasse between two opposing experts! Over the years I made many good friends through my membership of this and the other committees in which I was involved, and I again thank the others for the work and devotion which they contributed to the work of the committees, and to the Shetland environment.

A sub-committee of SOTEAG was the monitoring committee which drew up a programme for the monitoring of both Sullom Voe and the more general environment of Shetland, and employed experts to carry out the actual work involved. Apart from the obvious potential oil pollution from spills, some of the more unusual threats which came to light were the introduction of ballast water from foreign ports, which could contain either heavy metals or organisms which could wipe out those naturally present in the voe, and chemicals in the anti-fouling paint used on the bottoms of these vast tankers which, believe it or not, could cause female whelks to change sex – now there's a thought! Mussels were used as the sampling organisms for contaminants which they filtered out, and lichen on dykes and tombstones were sampled to test for atmospheric pollution. I also learned that the humble 'yoag' is more properly addressed as *Modiolus modiolus*, and after the *Esso Bernicia* incident, when bunker oil was spilled into the voe, SOTEAG and the monitoring committee learned to their cost that Shetland sheep eat seaweed on the shoreline.

Two other committees had also been established, with the special remit to look at the prevention of oil spills and the necessary action to be taken in the event of a spill. One of these was the Industry Oil Spill Advisory Committee (INOSAC) which was chaired by the terminal management and was responsible for prevention and control of spills within the terminal, and the other, the Sullom Voe Oil Spill Advisory Committee (SVOSAC), was responsible for the prevention of and dealing with spills outwith the terminal and, importantly, throughout Shetland. This was chaired by the director of ports and harbours, Captain George Biro, who was succeeded by Captain Bert Flett. The director of construction, Billy Smith, having control of the resources and staff of his organisation, and myself, were members of this committee.

A great deal of pre-planning took place into the possibility of oil spills and the resources required to clean up the result, but no one had any conception of the actual problems which would come to light until the huge spill from the *Esso Bernicia* on 30th December, 1978. This was around midnight in dead of winter, pitch dark and with snow on the ground. The oil which escaped was heavy bunker oil – from a tank on the vessel which ruptured on contact with part of a jetty – not any oil associated with terminal operations. The bunker oil more-or-less solidified and was virtually impossible to collect in any previously considered appropriate manner. Following this episode, huge amounts of money were spent on new equipment and on the provision of booms to be deployed at environmentally sensitive areas in the event of another spill. One of these sites is at the end of Voxter Voe, between Brae and Scatsta, where a yellow buoy can be seen in the middle of the voe, and concrete piers on either side where the boom will be deployed in an incident.

During the early part of the oil era Shetland was very fortunate in having the services, experience, and acumen of one of its sons who had risen through the ranks to become a senior member of the Esso Oil Company. Having worked as an engineer at the Malakoff slipway in Lerwick, then commissioned in the Royal Engineers during World War Two, John H. Manson had recently retired as chairman of an Institute of Petroleum sub-committee on the safety of oil and gas pipelines, an influential body in the energy industry. Born and brought up in Knab Road, John was a close friend and almost-neighbour of the then convener, Edward Thomason, so when Edward realised that John could be of immense help to Shetland he made overtures to him to come north again. John had apparently, in the past, maintained the position that he would not be coming back to Shetland "until oil was found at the back of Bressay"! Obviously this had now happened so his excuse had gone.

So, John duly arrived on the scene in 1972, and no words of mine can overemphasise the contribution he made on the prolonged and diverse negotiations which went on for years between the local authority and the oil industry representatives at meetings of the Sullom Voe Association. The fact that he was made secretary of SVA shows the respect in which John was held by both sides.

I cannot pass on without relating a story, told to me by John himself, regarding an occasion when he was asked by the chief executive, Ian Clark, to take some high ranking members of the British Ports Council to Sullom Voe to show them the facilities. Somewhere near Sella Ness the self-drive car got a puncture and John opened the boot to look for the spare wheel and tools. He was engaged in this when a car containing three or four local boys from the Sullom Voe shellfish factory stopped and asked what the problem was. John said that he had never had to jack up a Ford before and was not sure where the lifting points were situated. The response he got was, "Weel, for a start, it's a Vauxhall!" Then, seeing John with the jack in his hand, the leader said, "Na, we'll no budder wi' yun," and the three boys just put their backs to the car and lifted it while the extra man changed the wheel. The visitors watched amazed! It should be explained that John had spent so many years out of Shetland that his accent had been tempered to an extent that he could appear to be not of Shetland extraction. He therefore said, in his best 'sooth' accent, "Thenks awfully, cheps," climbed into the car and drove off, hoping that he had not been recognised as a thick Shetlander!

One of the first projects in which I was involved with John was in connection with the ballast water treatment facilities which were proposed to be provided by BP at the terminal. The purpose of these works was to reduce to an acceptable level the amount of oil in any water being discharged into Yell Sound. Not having sufficient knowledge or expertise fully to understand the various different stages which take place in such facilities, I suggested that we might be shown similar facilities in operation at a convenient BP terminal. Soon after, I was rather surprised to be invited to turn up at Sumburgh airport with my passport prior to leaving for a tour of the oil terminal at Mongstad in Norway. Being partly owned by BP it turned out that this was the nearest similar process to the one proposed for Sullom Voe. Together with Mike Fenwick, John Manson and industry representatives, we flew in the industry 'King Air' aircraft to Bergen, collected two self-drive cars and drove to Mongstad. There we had a thorough and detailed tour of the terminal which was, at that time, of a similar plan to Sullom Voe, in a deep-water inlet with short jetties. Then it was back to Bergen overnight and next morning we flew from Bergen across the Hardanger Vidda to Gothenburg in Sweden to see the treatment plant at the refinery there. Then it was on to Edinburgh for a meeting with officials from the planning department of the Scottish Office. That was a fairly long day, but when out for a stroll in Princes Street I heard some rather interesting jazz music coming from a club, and went to investigate. It was, in fact, Ronnie Scott's group with Ron Mathewson on bass, but there were no spare tickets. While standing at the door I was aware of someone coming up the stairs and this turned out to be none other than Peerie Willie Johnson who had arranged to meet Aly Bain who had tickets for them both!

During the construction phase, both at the terminal and at Norscot in Lerwick, invitations were received from both organisations for dinner parties at the Town Hall in the weeks before Christmas. Each seemed to vie with the other to produce a more exotic menu and wine, orchids for the ladies and cigars for the men were not in short supply. As the construction phase neared an end, or at least a slowdown, the accountants moved into operation and the excesses of the earlier years became fewer and fewer. There were still dinner parties, and sometimes lunches, and it was at one of these that a rather amusing incident occurred. Meg and I had been invited to a lunch, and at each table there was a representative of BP as host. Meg engaged in conversation with our host and asked if he had been long in Shetland. She was somewhat taken aback by the reply, "Does du no ken me, Meg?" This was none other than Andy 'Spud' Thomson, acting in his official capacity.

There were so many Welshmen at the terminal at one time that they were termed the 'Sullom Taffia'. A celebratory St David's Day dinner was held in the restaurant in the 'Planets' in Mounthooly Street, with a Welsh rugby player as the guest speaker. As you can imagine there was a great deal of hilarity, especially among the Welsh-speaking fraternity, which included the terminal manager, Tom Harris, from Anglesey. The chap sitting opposite me did not appear to speak Welsh so I spoke to him across the table during a lull and to my astonishment discovered that he was Jack Pottinger whom I had last encountered in my classes at the Infant and Central schools.

More changes were to take place in 1974 with the reorganisation of local government in Scotland. Although the changes were perhaps not so noticeable in Shetland which remained an 'all purpose' authority, than on the mainland where there were different functions for the regions and districts, there certainly were major changes so far as the personnel were concerned. Zetland County Council and Lerwick Town Council were amalgamated into Shetland Islands Council with a new crest and new letterheads. There were also new departments and new titles for the heads of departments who, in some instances, including myself, had to reapply for their posts.

For some reason, the powers that be had decided that the implementation of the housing legislation, which had been carried out by my department throughout the dull days of the early 1960s and the upsurge from 1968 including the early traumatic years of oil, should be removed and formed into a separate department. Furthermore, they had also decided that having removed housing from the duties, the department would now take on responsibility for weights and measures, including the Petroleum Spirit Regulations. So far as the chief inspector of weights and measures, Stanley Henry, and myself were concerned, there was no justification whatever for these changes which lumped together two departments which had virtually no common ground. However, the die was cast and Stanley and I had to apply for the post of director of environmental health and control.

There were other applicants, but the final choice apparently fell between the two of us and I was fortunate enough to be the successful candidate. The name of the department then changed to environmental health and consumer protection. The staff of the department now consisted of myself as director and, in the environmental health section Alan Blackburn as depute, David Okill as qualified assistant and Jim Barr as milk and food hygiene officer. In the weights and measures section, now called trading standards, there were Sam Steadman as chief trading standards officer, Alan Armstrong as assistant and Keith Robertson as trainee. Each section had secretarial staff, Marion Hunter and Doreen Johnson. At first there were problems as one section was operating from 92 St Olaf Street whilst the other was at 3 Commercial Road. Soon, however, arrangements were made for the environmental health section to vacate 92 St Olaf Street and occupy vacant rooms at 3 Commercial Road. This took some complicated planning as specialist requirements had to be met for trading standards legislation and, for the first time, we were able to have a proper laboratory for the milk and food hygiene officer.

The staff of Environmental Health and Consumer Protection, 1974: D. C. Smith, A. C. Blackburn, Dave Okill, Doreen Johnson, Sam Steadman, Keith Robertson, Jim Barr, Alan Armstrong, Marion Hunter.

Despite the two completely different disciplines I have to say that I was delighted with the way in which the members of staff integrated with one another, and I like to think that I ran a happy and efficient department from 3 Commercial Road for the next 15 years, during which there were several changes in the staff, mainly clerical.

The next problem arose in 1977 when the director of housing went on holiday to Australia and did not return. There seemed to be some delay in advertising for a replacement, but I was not prepared for the outcome of a summons to the office of the chief executive, by then Mike Gerard, in the Town Hall. Having run the housing department for many years until reorganisation, it now seemed that the chief executive wished me to take on these additional duties once more. Furthermore, the proposition was that my salary would be increased by, believe it or not, £500 per annum in respect of the additional responsibility and if I did not accept then my post would be advertised in the national press!

I went home in something of a turmoil but I really had no choice in the matter. I certainly did not wish to leave my post in the department which I had built up into its present form over so many years. Also, I had actually worked as acting director of housing until the first director was appointed in 1976 and I knew the staff in that department who had operated in the burgh of Lerwick for many years.

I therefore accepted the proposition, and my title became director of protective services and housing. The housing section moved into an adjoining room in Harbour Street with internal access so all sections were now combined within the one building. At that time the staff of the housing section comprised Willie Henderson as depute, Eileen Hutchison as administrative officer and Grace Sutherland, secretary. Later they were joined by Albert Slater as homeless persons officer and Jimmy Russell, clerk of works.

Mentioning homeless persons reminds me of an incident which happened long before that legislation was enacted. Dr Black was medical officer of health and a young couple turned up at his home one evening to say that they had been evicted by his parents and had nowhere to go. Dr Black told them that he certainly had a vacant house available, but that it was at the former Collafirth schoolhouse in Delting, in those days just about as remote a site as could be found in Shetland. Once the implications of the offer had sunk in, the young man said, "Collafirth! We're no goin' dere, we'll just go hom' again." Problem solved, and could they not all have been so easy?

Many of the people I had to interview in regard to housing matters were genuinely having problems, some more serious than others, and I always found it beneficial to let them have their say before making a judgement as to the merits of each case. There were, however, many 'chancers', particularly during the construction phase of the Sullom Voe terminal and the ancillary facilities in Lerwick and elsewhere. My department would get an urgent phone call to come to a house which was leaking badly during heavy rain, only to find that the occupier had been dowsing the walls with water in a vain attempt to jump the housing queue.

My first encounter with so-called 'hippies' was when I was called to the wartime bunkers at the Green Head at the north entrance to Lerwick harbour. A community had set up home there, no water, no power, no drainage, no facilities whatsoever, and they were hoping to earn some money from making candles. Given the Shetland weather, they did not maintain their occupation for long and I often wonder if the strange smell in the air was entirely from the production of candles. In fact, years later, I actually asked the local constabulary if the members of my department could be given some training in perceiving whether drugs were being used in a property as we were visiting sub-standard properties more often than any other department and could have passed on any information gained. However, this was apparently not considered beneficial and nothing more was heard.

Two more clients come to mind. One, a very large Irishman, was berating myself and Gussie Angus, depute director of the social work department, for not giving him a house in a particular area. When he realised that we were not going to be browbeaten he then threatened to bring the 'heavy mob' who would very soon dispose of both of us in their customary explosive manner. Needless to say, we are both still here and presume that the threat has now passed.

The second case was that of a chap from the central belt who was continually getting into trouble with the law for committing senseless crimes which were obviously carried out by him. During one of his several sojourns at 'Her Majesty's Pleasure' we found that he had been keeping a dog under the floor of the council house he shared with his wife. This was contrary to his missive of let so he was advised that the dog would be removed. Shortly after, I received a letter from one of HM Prisons stating that if I harmed one hair of the dog he would kill me (or words to that effect) when he was released! It so happened that I had been at a meeting in Aberdeen and was coming home on the 'plane when I noticed the said miscreant sitting handcuffed to a warder in the seat opposite me. He immediately waved his free hand and said, "I'm sorry, mister, I didn'y really mean it, OK?" In fact, a few days after he was released he came to the office and asked to see me. When he came into my office he asked if I could lend him "a quid for a cup of tea and game of snooker at the Mission"! I duly complied and he returned the quid the following day, sourced from I knew not where, and forbore to enquire.

CHAPTER FOURTEEN

A growing family

DURING this time, the family had obviously been growing up, both in stature and capabilities. To our great joy and satisfaction all three were deeply involved in sport, Gordon to the point of obsession in some instances. He played football for the school, Junior Rangers, Spurs, and the inter-county team of which he was captain on two occasions. He also played badminton and was Shetland senior men's champion at the age of 17, as the result of many evenings spent in St Clement's Hall.

Richard was also an excellent footballer and badminton player, and a very good swimmer, but he played for fun rather than having the killer instinct which seemed to take over Gordon whenever he competed. Richard's main input of late has been coaching a very successful junior team through the various age-groups involved.

Jill also swam very competently and partnered Gordon at badminton, although she complains that she never got a chance to return a shuttlecock because he was always behind her shouting "MINE"! Jill's crowning glory has, however, been her addiction to hockey. She is the possessor of five caps for playing for Shetland in the junior inter-county team, and no less than 29 caps (so far!) for playing for Shetland in the senior inter-county team, certainly a record as I write. She has also captained the Shetland inter-county hockey team more than once and we have had both the Hamilton and Milne Cups on our sideboard, albeit on separate occasions, when she and Gordon respectively captained the winning hockey and football teams.

In fact, since I wrote that paragraph last year, she has achieved her goal, having been once more selected for the team and gaining her 30th senior cap, and, to crown her success, she was appointed captain of the 2009 Shetland senior inter-county hockey team. This, in my opinion, was a fitting tribute to the dedication and effort which she has contributed to the sport over so many years.

Unfortunately the result was a win for Orkney and marks Jill's retirement from the inter-county scene but I would not be surprised if her voice was not heard from the touchline for a year or two yet!

I am delighted to report that our grandchildren have continued the tradition, being involved in a series of sports including football, badminton, hockey, fencing, volleyball, cycling, and swimming. Finding time for homework has always been a problem, but the results achieved by these young athletes are proving that it is possible to relax, have fun and still 'produce the goods'!

Gordon lives in Airdrie, near Glasgow, with his wife Margo and her son Steven from a previous marriage. Gordon is operations manager for the large haulage firm J.G. Russell.

The family at 55 King Harald Street, 1982.

Richard and Yvonne have three children, David (22) as I write, having recently graduated in accountancy at Glasgow University. Kate (21) in her final year at Edinburgh University aiming for primary teaching, and Robert (17) still here at the Anderson High School. Richard, until recently a technician with Open Reach Telecommunications, is now a technical officer with Hjaltland Housing Association.

Jill and Phil Hibbert have two, Paul (17) and Megan (16), both at Brae High School where Jill is principal teacher of physical education.

But to step back in time, our first holiday away from Shetland with all the family (then aged nine, seven and four), was in 1964 when we went to visit Marie and Wally who had by then moved to Preston in Lancashire. Wally was

Our extended family at Gordon's wedding to Margo, 16th March, 2007. From left: Richard, Paul, Jill, Meg, Megan, Gordon, Margo, Kate, Yvonne, me, Robert, David.

still employed by the Ministry of Civil Aviation and had been posted to that area in connection with air traffic control. These were the days before television and probably one of the best family holidays we ever had because everything was new and exciting for the younger members, and their excitement was infectious for us. Firstly the voyage on the old *St Clair*, then seeing the first double-decker bus in Aberdeen, a steam train near Stonehaven, trees, the Forth road bridge under construction above us as we crossed on the ferry to South Queensferry, and Edinburgh Zoo with all the exotic animals. All of these are now familiar sights and no longer provide any thrill or even great interest. We had a Ford Popular at the time and, with no windscreen washers, the journeys down the old A9 and back were rather uncomfortable with the number of trucks throwing up spray in the wet conditions. However, we survived, even carrying back our first 'Bush' television, tied on to the roof rack, wrapped in plastic sheets. Since then we have visited at least once a year and often twice, latterly, when family members were at college or university, in order to visit, feed and provide monetary refreshment for their diminishing 'student' resources, Edinburgh and Glasgow being convenient 'half-way houses' between Aberdeen and the Preston area.

Marie, although having been in the land of the dark satanic mills for more than forty years, can still be as broad Shetland in her speech as when she left. Having four Shetland sisters-in-law, Wally makes great play on having to endure the dialect during the visits of all these females. He particularly makes a point of noticing how often the word 'yun' is used in the conversation, and if one stands back and considers this, he really has a point: wha' is yun, what's yun, yun's yun, yun's enough, wha' wid wear yun? and so on, *ad infinitum*.

As time passed and the family no longer wished to accompany us, our holidays became a bit more adventurous. One year we went with Wally and Marie to the Loire Valley in France. I fear that repetitive castles and cathedrals are not my scene and for me the most interesting part was the area in Normandy which featured on 'D' Day, and I enjoyed seeing the Bayeux tapestry where, needless to say, we met a girl from Whalsay and her husband.

Thereafter, our thoughts were turned more and more in an easterly direction. After the arrival of Derrick Herning and my release from things

Russian I had a notion of trying another language which one could actually use. Latin was all very well for derivatives but not much else, and my schoolboy higher French had not impressed the inhabitants of the various chateaux – or anyone else for that matter! I therefore began to study Norwegian at evening classes at the Anderson High School and, in 1981, I managed to obtain an 'O' level which has proved very useful and beneficial over the intervening years.

After finishing with the Up-Helly-A' committee in 1968 I was able to join another organisation which had attracted me for as long as I can remember. I refer to Lerwick Brass Band, of which my uncle Wilfred had been a staunch member for many years in the past. When guizer jarl, one can choose the music to be played before the light-up while the jarl and squad march 'up the ranks' between the squads with their unlit torches. I had always associated the march 'The Stein Song' with Up-Helly-A', but it was also well known as one of the tunes played at the picture house when the audience was leaving, and a good tune into the bargain. I therefore asked bandmaster Bobby Burgoyne if he could get that march for me, which, after some difficulty, he did, and I went proudly 'up the ranks' to 'my' tune! Still interested in music, I therefore went to the band-room and asked if I could join. There was a vacancy for a trombonist so that is why I started on that instrument, and am still striving for some vague approach to perfection. Sadly, several faces from those early days are no longer with us, notably Bobby Burgoyne, 'Peerie Frankie' Sinclair and John Allan. There have been many changes in personnel over the years, but now, at the beginning of 2009, the band is as healthy and strong as it has ever been during my membership, with many young members.

In 1985/6 there was a big fund-raising effort with a view to the band travelling to Norway to play in our 'twin town' of Måløy. With our own bus from Leask's, and Ian Bruce as driver, we set off for Bergen on the old *Norrona*, together with parents, wives, girlfriends and representatives from Shetland Islands Council. Ian then drove us via Voss and Balestrand to Måløy, on roads which bear no resemblance to the almost motorways of today. A few days of concerts and festivities, then it was back to Bergen for a concert in the veterans' club, 'Kronstad', where we met several veterans who had been in Shetland in the various services during World War Two. Back on board the

Norrona for the voyage home we had a burial at sea, with full brass band honours, for Tom Bulley's self-deploying umbrella as we sailed towards the fast setting sun in the west.

I think that it must have been this trip which infected me – and Meg – with the overwhelming 'itch' to return to Norway, again and again! In 1987 and '88, the *St Clair* made weekend tours to Bergen, leaving Lerwick at midnight on Friday and returning in time to sail for Aberdeen again on the Monday evening. One of these tours coincided with the 17th of May parade when the population of Norway celebrates independence from Sweden, and in Bergen the parade is second only to Oslo. It is a wonderful, colourful, noisy and cheerful occasion with flags and national costumes everywhere. Veterans, soldiers, sailors, airmen, students, parents with infants in prams, and brass bands everywhere, it is a scene not easily forgotten. Some of us were invited to join a local family in their home during the afternoon and we were well entertained to the traditional dishes of rømmegrøt and spekeskinke, a sort of porridge and smoked ham – separately of course. In the evening there was a dance in the bar of the *St Clair* and we were joined by a veteran of the 'Shetland Bus', Rolf Nordhus, well known in Scalloway and elsewhere in Shetland, who was the life and soul of the party and exhausted a succession of dancing partners. We met Rolf many times after this occasion but, like so many other veterans of the war, he is no longer alive.

I retired in September 1989 after exactly 40 years with 'Da Coonty' and persuaded Meg that an excellent way of celebrating the event would be to take the famous 'Hurtigrute' coastal voyage from Bergen to Kirkenes in the far north of Norway. I am delighted to say that she agreed and we sailed from Bergen on the 18th June, 1990, returning on the 4th July, after 11 days and an unforgettable trip, having spent midsummer near the North Cape.

Up until then we had either not heard of Shalder Coach tours, or at least not thought of them as anything other than the Scalloway bus service. We were soon to learn otherwise and since 1992 Meg and I have been regular passengers, whenever possible, on Andrew Morrison's enchanting tours of Norway. I am almost reluctant to use the word 'passengers' as those on the bus are really like a family group and treated as such by Andrew, his wife Davina and, more and more these days, by their son Morris. Starting on the old black and white buses, and through to the new magnificent state-of-the-art coaches, we have been driven thousands of feet above sea level at Dalsnibba overlooking Geiranger, and hundreds of feet below sea level through tunnels to the islands near Ålesund. Often with many former fellow-passengers we have been from the top of the Holmenkollen ski-jump to Liset in the south, to Vestkapp, the spectacular Lofotens and Nordkapp, and revisiting these places is just as interesting as seeing them for the first time. I have also been able to reunite with many veterans and see places associated with the links between Shetland and Norway during World War Two. Meg and I have been on 18 tours with Andrew to Norway (so far), but the future looks rather bleak as, with the withdrawal of the *Norrona* and the end of the link to Norway from Newcastle, there is no logical route to get a bus from Shetland across the mere 180 miles of North Sea between us and Bergen.

One non-Norwegian tour was to Faroe, Iceland and Greenland in 1998, but because of the long sea crossings, Meg decided to do some gardening (aka 'sense') instead. This was a really unusual and unforgettable tour in many ways, not least because of our Icelandic guide who took us to 'mountains which are not there' and through a tunnel which he insisted did not exist, and which we were then advised to pass through with our eyes closed – Andrew asked if he could keep his open! The differing terrain of the three islands was enthralling, from the flat black lava fields and spectacular waterfalls of Iceland, to the geometric shape of the Faroese hills, and the barren rocks of south-east Greenland, at the settlement of Amassalik, where one can walk among the icebergs stranded on the shores of the fjord in shirt-sleeve order in unbroken sunshine.

We did actually miss out on two years with Andrew. In 1996 we went to New Zealand to reunite with members of the 'Islesburgh Smith' clan who had emigrated there in the 1920s. Travelling from Auckland to Palmerston North and Wellington in North Island, and Picton to Christchurch to Invercargill in South Island, we spent six weeks in the opposite ends of the earth, a lot of the time being driven around in a 1927 open-topped Austin 12/4 Clifton Tourer which was a wonderful experience in itself. The second 'missing' year was 2001

Richard, Jill and Gordon, 1993.

when Meg (always the one with the common sense) decided that we needed a new porch at Cliff House more than we needed a holiday – she has now, in 2009, been forgiven.

All these Norwegian holidays added to my interest in the language, and even if I was too unsure of myself to launch out into casual conversations, it was very helpful to be able to recognise names and types of premises, road signs and the like. On each of our holidays I took the opportunity to visit the local 'Antikvariat', second-hand bookshop, and look for books associated with Shetland and/or the 'Shetland Bus' operations, and over the years I have amassed a large collection. Some of these I have translated on my computer, purely for my own interest, but I also find the exercise very useful when I meet any of the surviving veterans as the conversation tends to turn to Nazis, bombs, saboteurs, depth-charges and the like, which usually produces a fairly obvious lack of interest from any females in the company!

CHAPTER FIFTEEN

The move

IHAVE taken the title of this chapter from a Bell's Brae Primary School workbook which was used by Richard and featured a farmer called Old Lob and a goat by the name of Mr Grumps. However, this move was a rather more traumatic experience in that it concerned a change of dwelling for us, and my leaving the house in which I had been born, for the final time.

As I have described already, 55 King Harald Street was a big house, but on four levels and not in the least conveniently arranged internally. As our family gradually grew up and left home to pursue their own lives, Meg and I realised that this house was far too big for the two of us. Early in 1984 we began to look in the local press for alternatives, but having had the open aspect facing across the valley to the Town Hall as our everyday view, we did not want to be shut in by other properties. Meg, in particular, being a very definite 'country-life' lass, needed as wide open a vista as possible, but this is not all that easy in any town. On the other hand, as a 'toony' I did not want to be too far from the harbour or the sight of boats (one never knows what might be going on out of sight), so taking into account these rather varied restrictions our choice was a bit limited.

Anyway, we eventually saw an advert for the sale of a house called Cliff House, at 3 Montfield. Although my brother Jim and his wife Cathy had lived for several years in Bon Accord at 1 Montfield, I must admit that the presence of a property next door had never registered. We went and had a look at the property and liked what we saw so made an offer which in due course was accepted. The next problem, of course, was the sale of '55' and this took a lot longer than we would have wished, requiring a bridging loan and suchlike expensive overheads. During the intervening period we undertook the work necessary to transform Cliff House to our own requirements.

Built in 1951, Cliff House was a bungalow with a large partly-floored loft. Situated high over the west part of the town, it has magnificent views over the south entrance to the harbour, Bressay, the north harbour, Nesting, Whalsay, and even Fetlar on a fine day. Boats for me and wide open spaces for Meg. It had been most recently occupied by people involved in the oil industry and their views on decor did not really correspond with ours, so a great deal of magnolia emulsion was applied to the woodchip wallpaper. Heating was by 'Nightstor' heaters and the whole property required rewiring. One problem was that all the internal walls were solid concrete block, so the electricians had some difficulties to overcome. However, in time we were able to move in and Meg could appreciate the benefit of being able to 'Hoover' the whole house with only one change of plug instead of previously carrying the machine up and down three flights of stairs.

Access to the house was from the lower road at Montfield and then by a flight of steps to the front of the house. There was also a garage with very difficult access. The then occupiers of Bon Accord had come to an agreement

Cliff House, 1984.

151

with John Tulloch, the owner of the surrounding land and house at Inches, whereby they had made a road up to the back of their house, but this stopped at the stone wall which formed the boundary of the back garden of Cliff House. I approached John, a long time friend of the family, with a view to extending the road into the back garden to give us vehicle access, and pedestrian access without steps. Permission was granted. We had a large tarred area laid and Richard and I built a new garage, so life began anew.

Subsequently we built on a sunroom, double glazed throughout, installed cavity fill and loft insulation and floored the loft to give Meg a work area for her sewing and art work, and room for my computer station and 'toys' as they are described by others.

Finally, we were among the first to have district heating installed with radiators everywhere including the loft, so I think that we are just about as comfortable as possible.

When we moved in, the garden boasted one tulip and a sea of honeysuckle which had fallen off the wall and spread on to the grass area, not really classed as a lawn. Now, despite the wild winds on top of the hill and with the help of shelter belts, Meg, being the horticultural expert, has transformed the whole place with trees, hedges and flower beds.

Of course, this is not the only garden which Meg has produced and nurtured. In 1975, being a bit fed up with life 'i' da toon', she fell on the idea of us having a summer house at the 'ness and bought a plot of land at Durigarth, near Skelberry, off the road from Robin's Brae to Spiggie. The property comprised two large grass areas surrounded by stone walls, a shed which had been a smithy and a large roofless two-storey house in a ruinous condition. There were a few stunted willows in the lower area, and the house was full of old fencing wire and rubbish – as the estate agent might have said, 'ripe for development'.

On our next safari to Preston we bought a small caravan and towed it back to Aberdeen and home, then used it on holidays in different parts of Shetland, as well as somewhere for a base when at Durigarth, known by the younger family members as 'Durriduck'. The boys took great delight in demolishing the stone walls of the porch and we cleared the house and took away flagstones to make a paved area in front. This was in 1981, about the time when the construction firm Trentham's was engaged in widening the east-west runway at Sumburgh. When the contract was finished they offered for sale various huts and caravans rather than shipping them south again. Meg had firstly intended to rebuild the old house, but was eventually convinced that the gable walls were cracked and unstable, so then thought about building a new house there. I have to admit that I was completely opposed to that suggestion as I considered one house was quite sufficient for our needs, and being only about 20 minutes from Lerwick there was no justification for building a house which would inevitably stand empty for the greater part of the year.

After some 'debate' a compromise was reached and she bought one of the large residential caravans which was transported to the site and placed on the paved area. Anchorages were constructed to secure the caravan, water, drainage and electricity were connected, and Durigarth was once more ready for occupation. Over the intervening years a lot of work has been put in to produce the changes and improvements which are now evident. The caravan has been transformed into a permanent chalet, there are many trees of various kinds, and Meg has worked tirelessly to cultivate and nurture flowers in various parts of the garden. The big grass area has been an ideal football and camping ground for the younger members of the family, but now the fleshpots of Lerwick, computer games and the like have removed a lot of the former magic.

For a time we grew vegetables, breaking out the soil with a 'Merry Tiller', but eventually that was discontinued. The ever-present hordes of rabbits made the effort to produce vegetables a waste of time and now they are making every effort to eat as many of the flowers and young shrubs as possible. Dozens can be counted in the surrounding fields, and instead of burrowing under the walls they now just run up the outside face and jump down inside. No one seems to care a jot, so the problem can only exacerbate unless something in the 'myxi' line appears – I can't see many tears being shed if that were to happen.

Meg's favourite therapeutic relaxation is building and repairing stone walls but having levelled and tidied up many of the old walls, there are still some which are not pleasing to her artistic eye. Certainly pleasing to the eye is the sight of Bertie, the neighbouring crofter, cutting his field of bere with a reaper/binder and then seeing the sheaves standing in the evening sunshine – a rare sight these days.

I am still of the opinion that one house and one garden is enough for folk who are aged 80 and over. As a sop to my inabilities, Meg bought a sit-on mower which is a huge benefit in controlling the half an acre (seems more) of grass, although this is being done more and more by Richard and Robert. I am sorry that I cannot settle to the idea that we are less capable of doing what was quite reasonable 10 or 20 years ago, and fairly soon the fact will have to be faced that the proper upkeep of Durigarth is too big and too exhausting a project for us. But, likely, "Na, na, no yet," as the regular helmsman said to the relieving skipper of the *Earl*, when ordered to change course.

I suppose that, if this is the only bone of contention in the 56th year of our marriage, it will likely last a bit longer.

In 1975 I was approached with a view to becoming the first chairman of the Parent-Teacher Association at the Anderson High School. Jill was still a pupil so at least I had an interest, and agreed. At the inaugural meeting, Provost Eric Gray nominated me and said that I was in the audience but, looking round, was rather baffled to find that I was nowhere to be seen. The problem was that for many years I had sported a beard, but in the period since he had last seen me I had shaved it off, and was rather incognito. This was a position which I held and enjoyed as long as Jill remained a pupil.

CHAPTER SIXTEEN

Meanwhile ... back in the office

THERE are so many different problems associated with housing, from simple complaints about lack of maintenance, condensation, problem neighbours in relation to compatibility, noise, or just general behaviour, to gross overcrowding, single parenthood and so-on. The sale of council houses had certainly reduced the public housing stock, but I always felt that the majority of tenants who bought their houses intended to remain in them in any event. About this time there was also concern about the state of many of the council houses and a programme of major repair and refurbishment was discussed and recommended to the council. One problem for the officials was that the housing stock ranged from the stone-built houses in Lerwick from 1919, to relatively recent wooden houses in rural areas. Many of the oldest properties were in better condition than those of more recent age, but the older houses were out-dated so far as items such as facilities and insulation were concerned. There were complaints from councillors representing tenants in the older houses that priority was being given to newer properties, and counter complaints that the old houses were at least wind and watertight which could not be said for many others.

There was also extreme pressure on the department and the housing committee in relation to finding accommodation for homeless persons, of whom more and more were accumulating, despite the heroic efforts of the staff of the housing department and in particular Albert Slater, the homeless persons officer. As a retired policeman, Albert was the ideal person for this thankless task, patient, thorough, but not easily 'conned' by any of the often bizarre excuses which were presented to him. I, myself, had an instance where a lady who had just arrived in Shetland came to my office seeking emergency accommodation. She suggested that her husband held a position of some importance as a member of a well-known organisation, and this therefore should entitle her to have priority. I think she was a bit surprised when I made it very clear that I was not a member of the said organisation and showed her the door.

I found that there was more and more pressure on both the department and myself, and that I was beginning to 'take my work home'. I eventually requested that the chief executive suggest to the council that a separate housing department, with its own director, should be re-established and was very relieved when this was approved and this burden was removed.

Two very interesting groups in which I was involved were associated with infectious diseases and food poisoning. During my early days in the office I was often called upon to visit houses where there had been a case of tuberculosis, an outbreak of scarlet fever or some such affliction. I do not know what procedure is followed these days but, 'way back then, in relation to TB the advice was to open all the windows and doors and let the fresh air do the work. This, however, did not always satisfy the occupiers left in the property, especially in mid-winter, and I was invariably asked to fumigate the property. That was also always the case with scarlet fever, measles, whooping cough and so on. This was done by placing tins containing a chemical mixture, which produced formaldehyde gas when water was added, as a disinfectant. The thing to remember was always to start with the tin furthest from the door, but sometimes the chemicals in the tin would not perform and required a second application which called for fairly rapid exits on occasion. This procedure also seemed effective when I encountered fleas in a property, which was not at all uncommon in the early days. Fleas seemed to have an affinity for me rather than anyone else present, and an early bath to 'float them off' was always a good move. I have not encountered one (or vice-versa) for some years now so maybe improved hygiene has eradicated them – I hope I'm not speaking too soon.

In the early days there were also two local outbreaks of typhoid fever, one as a result of a contaminated well and the other from a food premises. Later, of course, there was the extensive Aberdeen outbreak when several students had arrived home from Aberdeen University and had to be traced, any contacts recorded, and instructions given to report to their GP if any unusual symptoms appeared. For this investigation both the medical officer of health and myself had to be inoculated.

One of the groups which I, together with the county sanitary inspector from Orkney, was a founder member of was the Communicable Diseases Control Group which was established and chaired by Dr Smith, the then chief bacteriologist at Aberdeen City Hospital laboratory. This is where all the milk and water samples from the two island groups were tested and Dr Smith realised that, by having the two of us cooperating with him, we could hopefully take pre-emptive action to prevent, as far as possible, any major outbreaks of communicable diseases by taking immediate action if he found any problematic results in the samples. This cooperation worked well and we established a rapport with the laboratory and its staff which was, so far as I am concerned, of immense value to Shetland. As time passed, this group was expanded to include medical officers of health and directors of environmental health from Aberdeen, Aberdeenshire, Moray and Kincardine, as well as animal health experts and specialists from Aberdeen Royal Infirmary and elsewhere. Meetings were held twice a year in Aberdeen and, apart from the agenda, it gave me an opportunity to discuss other matters of mutual interest with my colleagues.

It was, in fact, at one of these discussions that we, by chance, began to talk about food poisoning and its effects, and the conversation then turned to the fact that there were literally thousands of people employed offshore who were not covered by the regulations which controlled hygienic practices in food premises on shore.

Furthermore, if there was to be a major outbreak of food poisoning offshore, the patients would have to be evacuated by helicopter to the nearest available treatment facilities and, apart from Aberdeen which might be able to cope with a sudden major influx of sufferers, there was certainly not adequate extra hospital capacity in Lerwick, Kirkwall or any of the other potential reception areas. It seemed to us that the situation was sufficiently worrying to require an immediate approach to the medical representatives of the offshore oil industry. This was done and a working group was set up to take the matter further.

The group had the very unwieldy name of the Environmental Health Liason Group for the UK Continental Shelf, and consisted of the directors of environmental health for the areas most at risk, medical officers of health, senior staff from Aberdeen Royal Infirmary and the senior medical representatives from the main oil companies working in the northern North Sea. With input from each of the professions a code of practice was drawn up for hygienic practices in the supply, handling and processing of food to be consumed on the offshore installations. This was submitted to the UK Offshore Oil Association. Of course, this was actually only a recommended code of practice with no legal standing but, I am glad to say, during the time when I was chairman of the group it was accepted and put into practice.

During our discussions we held meetings in Peterhead, Aberdeen, Orkney and here in Shetland, which enabled the various members to see the different facilities and problems associated with each area. We were also taken to the Forties Bravo platform, off Aberdeen, by helicopter to examine the impressive catering facilities and equipment which was available on the giant steel structure. I think the most unnerving part of the trip was standing on the helideck, which had a lattice floor, looking down to the surface of the sea a mind-bending distance below!

My only other involvement with an oil rig was in connection with the issue of what is called a 'derat certificate'. Port health regulations require all vessels to have a deratisation certificate, renewed every six months, stating that it is free of rats and other vermin otherwise the ship had to be sent to an authorised port to be fumigated. In the early days of the oil era there was no port in Shetland which was authorised to issue such certificates, so an approach was made to the Scottish Office and authorisation was granted to Lerwick, which was taken to include Scalloway and Sullom Voe, with my department as the authorised signatory. This now meant that tankers and other vessels did not have to go to Aberdeen or the nearest available port for a vessel of that size, to have their certificates renewed. This work was, of course, right up Alan Blackburn's street and he really enjoyed rooting around the ships of all shapes and sizes and reminiscing with the officers and crews. Some of the tankers were really huge and I remember one which had a lift, with seven floors from engine room to the bridge, and there was a box on which the very small captain stood to see out of the bridge windows.

However, back to the oil rig, a message was received in the office that the oil rig 'Sovereign Explorer' was heading to Lerwick before being deployed offshore and would require a derat certificate. I had been sitting at the desk doing reports for days and decided to 'pull rank' and have an outing myself. I boarded one of the Maersk supply boats and found Neil Donald also there bound for the same destination. The rig was lying just off the north end of Bressay and when we arrived a 'basket' was lowered from a crane on the deck high above. To explain, this 'basket' was a sort of conical structure made of rope with a wooden floor. The 'passengers' stand on the outer rim of the floor and hang on to the outside of the rope network forming the cone. Neil and I duly attached ourselves as best we could and suddenly we shot vertically up to the crane, swung in over the side of the platform, and straight down on to the deck. How I wished that I was still at my safe and sound desk! I imagine that the crane driver was falling about with laughter at my face at least. This was in calm weather, just outside the harbour, and I could but think of the poor souls who had to board a rig in this way during a storm in the middle of the North Sea. Anyway, the inspection took place, the certificate was granted and I returned to the deck of the supply boat vowing that this was the last outing of this kind for me.

I found it strange that, as I began to look towards the few remaining years before retirement, things began to get more complicated and problematic instead of simpler, as I had expected. New legislation and changes to existing conditions seemed to be appearing by the day. Over the previous almost 40 years there had been remarkably few changes in the staff but each time there was change in the secretarial staff it took some time for the new incumbent to assimilate the filing regime of the department and even the phraseology of the director. More and more time seemed to be spent at meetings, including those of the management team which were held in the office and under the chairmanship of the chief executive. I found these meetings occasionally very useful as they gave an insight into the thought processes of the other directors, and sometimes even a glimpse into the convoluted connections between Shetland Islands Council and the oil industry. There is no doubt, in my mind, that there was an inner sanctum where many of the weighty considerations were discussed without the presence of several of the other departmental directors. In fact, at one particular meeting, myself, Billy Smith, the director of construction, and Pat Regan, the director of administration, were very nearly sacked for suggesting that far too much time was being spent on business connected with the oil industry to the detriment of the time being devoted to the county of Shetland, for which we were appointed and being paid. Pat had a wonderful phrase which I really must quote: "*I will offer you every kind of assistance short of actual help.*"

As time progressed there seemed to be more and more unrest and dissatisfaction creeping in among all staff, from secretaries to directors. With repeated job evaluations, time and motion studies, salary reviews and the like, to put it bluntly, the fun had gone out of the job, and I think I can say that it was the same, whatever job one held. I had been very happy in my work, perhaps most happy earlier on when I was able to get away from the office desk and meet folk all over the islands. There had been a great camaraderie between the various directors and the staff throughout the entire organisation and I am sure that this contributed to the trouble and strife-free manner in which our business was conducted. This now seemed to have gradually been eroded and jealousies in relation to salary gradings, and increases in staff were becoming more and more common. So far as I was concerned, perhaps one of the most surprising decisions taken was to abolish the post of director of administration. In the operation of my department every decision, every recommendation, every move, had to be carried out according to whichever 'act', 'order' or 'regulation' was being applied, and the person to whom any query had to be addressed or advice sought was the director of administration. Always a lawyer, he was the safeguard against possible legal action against the person seeking the advice, or the authority itself. In my view, the director of administration was second in importance only to the chief executive, although the director of finance might have had an opinion on that statement!

One other huge change for me was the retirement through ill health of my true and trusted colleague for more than 20 years, Alan Blackburn. Alan had been having trouble with his eyesight and despite repeated visits to Aberdeen Royal Infirmary for treatment the prognosis was not good so he decided to withdraw to his beloved garden at Blydoit. A great personality, Alan was always the life and soul of the office, with his descriptions of very recognisable folk as "the man with the dark brown voice," or "the man with the dogswool and oakum breeks"! He did not suffer fools gladly and, albeit a Liverpudlian, would pour scorn on the antics of 'soothmoothers'.

A new breed was entering into my profession, university BSc. graduates in environmental subjects. Given the ever more complicated scientific and pollution-control related legal requirements which were being introduced, it was evident that the training which I, for example, had undertaken in the 1950s was no longer adequate. One of these graduates, Martin Hall, was appointed to replace Alan as depute director and, in due course, he succeeded me as director of the department, while Dave Okill moved on and upwards to become the head of the Shetland branch of the Scottish Environment Protection Agency.

In any event, as I approached retirement there were dramatic changes both in departmental organisation and in committee structure. As I have said earlier, I am not at all convinced that these changes have brought any noticeable improvement in the operation of the authority since the 'old days', when each director reported to a separate committee which again was subservient to the final decision of the full council. It was also, in my opinion, far easier (maybe far too easy) to contact the appropriate official when the departments had a name which gave a clear idea of their function – roads, architects, planning or, for that matter, sanitary. So, having carried out my duties through the 'reigns' of five medical officers of health and six county clerks/chief executives, it was obviously time to retire, gracefully or otherwise, which I did on 30th September, 1989, exactly 40 years from the 3rd October,

1949, when I 'signed on'. My staff had organised a farewell party, with a cake in the appropriate shape of a toilet, and with that, it was off to 'civvy street'.

During the past 40 years I had enjoyed the privilege of meeting many highly qualified, highly skilled and highly entertaining people in many varied positions and situations. Certainly there had been times when matters arose or decisions were taken which made me feel unsettled, but that's life, and overall it had been a great experience. Later, someone asked me if I was missing life at the office, to which I replied, "Only the staff and the photocopier!"

All smiles on retirement day, 30th September, 1989.

CHAPTER SEVENTEEN

Retirement

WHAT have I achieved since I retired? A very good question. My aunt, Flora Campbell, had a very keen sense of humour and many years ago had a small booklet printed with the title 'What I know about Golf'. The contents were a series of blank pages and, looking back on the past 20 years or so, I am almost inclined to leave a blank page or two as well.

No sooner had I retired than I received a 'phone call asking if I would consider representing a certain area in Shetland as its councillor. This was not actually on my wish-list so I (politely, I hope) declined and have never regretted that decision.

Meg has been known to say, "What have we achieved today?" to which I invariably reply, "Nothing, but why do we *have* to achieve *anything*?"

I think that, in Meg's case and that of her four sisters, the 'achieving' theme stems from their mother who was perpetually on the move. While Jim was at the office as BEA superintendent at Sumburgh Airport, she ran the house, did all the outside chores, and brought up the family. The girls were indoctrinated never to sit 'hand idle' and, if there was nothing else requiring attention, the instruction was 'tak your wires' (knitting needles). From milking the cow, tarring roofs, turning eggs in the incubators and feeding hens, to carrying water from the well near Sumburgh Farm, not to mention work at the peat hill, there must have been days when there seemed to be insufficient hours available.

One story concerning the peat hill at Virdiefield deserves a mention. Wally, at that time Marie's fiancé, was 'hurlin' peats in a barrow from the 'grev' up to the road by means of a narrow plank. Mother Black was aware that he was going 'off the rails' and shouted, "Geen a bit ta sudderd, Wally," (go more toward the south), without thinking that, being from Lancashire, the coordinates for 'da sudderd' at Virdiefield might not be immediately apparent to the barrower. Fortunately, the journey was safely accomplished.

Having five daughters all with multiple Christian names, it is puzzling why each of them is more familiarly known by the name which begins with 'M' (Meg, Marie, Myrna, Mildred and Merle). This situation made it vitally important that when addressing a *billet-doux* to one of them, one did not merely write 'Miss M. Black' on the envelope. Having no boys in the family, Jim was left with the task of training the older girls in the rather unladylike pursuits of changing the wheels on the car or clearing a petrol choke by blowing through the pipe leading to the carburettor. When he went fishing he required someone on hand to steer the boat. He taught all of them to drive and probably other crofting-type tasks to which I am not privy.

When two male suitors appeared on the scene Jim must have thought that help was on hand. However, as you have read, Wally was not the most accomplished barrow-handler of all time, and I was very willing but 'haandless'. Jim was erecting a fence in the park and I offered to drive in some

The five Grutness sisters: Merle, Marie, Mildred, Myrna and Meg.

posts for him. Having stabilised the post, he gave me his treasured fencing maul and went off to do something else. I managed to drive the post in a few inches and decided to give it a real whack. Raising the maul over my head I brought it down with as much force as I could muster. Unfortunately, my 3-D vision is not accurate and when the head of the maul reached its target it was just beyond the top of the post. At that point the handle of the maul broke off and the head continued on its journey earthwards to make a crater in the ground. I was excused duties forthwith!

But the theme has certainly persisted in Meg who cannot sit 'hand idle' and over the years her artistic talents have produced many notable artworks, from her unmistakeable collages made with shells, bark, 'siggie' leaves and suchlike, to paintings and weavings. These, of course, have been produced while she was not involved in housework, cooking meals, dressmaking or other works associated with the several sewing machines which adorn our loft! This does not take into account her beloved passion of gardening, both in Lerwick and particularly at Durigarth, where there is also the therapeutic dry-stone walling. When she sits down in the evening (time permitting) she will either 'tak her wires' or do crossword puzzles while watching the very occasional programme on the television. Very proud of the fact that she cannot even switch on the computer, this gives her more time to do work "for the COMMON GOOD!", and jumping from the bed at unearthly hours in the morning she claims to do 'a day's work' before I surface.

I am very envious of her many talents. My lethargy and 'laid-back' approach to life must be a real pain to her. I am reminded of the attitude of a very good friend of ours who, when he thinks that something needs to be done, just sits down until the feeling wears off!

I am not particularly good with my hands so far as constructing anything is concerned, but potter round the house and garden doing 'make-do-and-mend' jobs. This normally occurs when I have been told that, "SOMETHING NEEDS TO BE DONE ABOUT…"

In turn, this removes me from one or other of my hobbies/priorities/obsessions which can occupy a large part of any available time. The one thing which any course on retirement fails to take into account is that there is no

Golden Wedding, 30th September, 2003.

such thing as retirement! There are not enough hours in the day for everything that still has to be done, at least not in my day.

Photography has always been a hobby of mine, as has stamp collecting and, since I retired, translating Norwegian wartime books. On one occasion I was translating a book about Bjørn Rørholt, a famous secret agent who was on his way to Trondheim to report on the movements of the German pocket-battleship *Tirpitz*. I read that he was staying in the Queen's Hotel here in Lerwick but was unable to leave until the stormy weather improved and one evening he awoke, shouting from a nightmare in which he was trapped and being bombed by the Germans. His companion calmed him down and it was later established that the nightmare had been caused by explosions which had happened during the course of the night. By checking the dates involved, it was really interesting to find out that this was the same night when I was at the Boys' Brigade and the mines exploded in Breiwick.

I also enjoy writing articles and, during the summer months, tour guiding, whenever an opportunity occurs. Meg and I also like to beachcomb, all around Shetland, looking for materials for her collages, and we have walked a fair bit, but have a lot of walks still on the books which hopefully may be accomplished while we are both reasonably fit and able. At the risk of being a bit repetitive, I will lay out a list of some of my time-consuming pursuits.

Before we went to Norway with Lerwick Brass Band in 1986 I bought a Panasonic video camera and that has almost been part of my life since then. The first camera was a 'full size' version which took tapes which played in the video player so it was bulky and heavy, no comparison whatever with the tiny 'miniaturised' versions available today. The quality of the results of the filming has improved as the size of the cameras has shrunk and the number of additional facilities and 'gizmos' now built into the works is unbelievable. I have used a succession of cameras to record the lives of our various grandchildren, starting with David in 1987, and the resulting tapes or DVDs give us great pleasure and amusement when we look back over the intervening years.

I have also made video recordings of all our holidays in Norway and elsewhere, and these are very useful *aide-memoires* if any question arises as to

Sandefjord, Norway, 2007.

where we were or who was there on a certain tour. Editing video tapes has also improved immeasurably with the introduction of digital editing programmes. In the early days, before digital, one seemed to need about four hands to be able to push, pull, turn or switch on and off all the knobs and slides which had to be adjusted. Now, with a touch of the 'mouse' on the computer, all is solved (I wish). My 'productions' are becoming reasonably proficient and I now show them to groups such as the SWRI and the Shetland-Norwegian Friendship Society.

I have always had an interest in geography and my stamp collecting interest began even before I went to school, when my father had his herring business and received an apparently immense amount of mail, particularly from Germany. I can remember him giving me a great bag full of stamps, many of which had been overprinted with '1 million marks' during the depression in Germany in the 1930s. When a stamp club was started by maths teacher, John Reid, in Class 1 at the Institute, I began to 'seriously' collect stamps. A lot of this was done through 'swops' of 'dupes' with other members, and begging used envelopes from people whom I knew had travelled and might be concealing some treasures of that type. I still have my original 'Stanley Gibbons' album, and several more which have been and are still being filled, although many of my sources are drying up as I have moved into the era of emails. I find it interesting to look through the old albums and see the never-ending changes which seem to take place in the names of countries which were in everyday use in my day at school – Kenya, Uganda and Tanganyika, Bechuanaland, Czechoslovakia – the list is endless. I have not been specific in my collections, attractive and interesting stamps are always the most collectable so far as I am concerned, and whenever in a foreign country I try to look for a few new additions.

A couple of years after I retired I received a note suggesting that local tour guides were being sought to accompany tourists on buses. The main idea was to replace guides who were coming to Shetland from elsewhere and who had little or no knowledge of Shetland, its history or culture. Bus drivers were relating instances of guides giving descriptions of Ronas Hill when pointing at the Ward of Bressay, and Jarlshof being discussed when passing through Fladdabister – no doubt highly enlightening to the uninitiated, but not what would today be called 'fit for purpose'! Having lived here virtually all of my life, and working for the local authority for 40 years in a job which took me to every road-end in the islands, I felt that I maybe had something to offer. A course of instruction was established by Shetland Enterprise and several of us attended and this has led to perhaps the most interesting 'extra mural' activity for me during the tourist season. It was quite amazing, so far as I was concerned, to find out just how little I knew about the history (that word again) of Shetland and the intricacies of the various ages of Jarlshof, but over the years 'practice makes perfect', or reasonably so, and I think that I can now face a bus load of tourists with relative confidence and leave them with enough information to instil a desire to return.

The problem with a place as small as Shetland is that, when a very large liner arrives there are problems accessing sufficient buses and guides to satisfy the needs of the shipboard tour operators. Another problem arises when the tourists are non-English speaking. A translator must then accompany the guide and while this can occasionally be a satisfactory option, the outcome often depends on the linguistic skills of the translator and the rapport between them and the guide. I was on one occasion instructed to "Wheesht!" by a Teutonic frau who insisted in reading from a brochure about Mousa when I was hoping to tell the visitors about Gulberwick. As a guide, I do get a lot of fun and enjoyment meeting all the various people on the buses. The different nations all have their differences in personality. As a Norwegian speaker, I get a lot of enjoyment out of the obvious interest Norwegians have in the links between our two countries and the linguistic similarities in the old Shetland dialect to Norwegian language.

It is a particular pleasure to meet veterans who escaped to Shetland when their country was invaded by Nazi Germany in April 1940. Many of them served in the Norwegian armed forces and were stationed here, so there are many stories told of those dark and exciting days. To mention only two who have become particular friends: Fredrik Kayser was one of the saboteurs who took part in the famous raid on the heavy water plant at Vemork, glamorised in the film *The Heroes of Telemark*, and Egil Johansen who, in 1941, tried with a friend to cross from Bergen to Shetland in a two-man kayak. Egil later served in the Royal Norwegian Air Force at Sullom Voe and returned for the unveiling of the 'Shetland Bus' monument in Scalloway in 2003. Sadly, as I write this, I have just learned from his daughter that Fredrik Kayser died last week at the age of 90, another loss to the list of surviving veterans.

American tourists are difficult to categorise. One of the easiest couriers with whom I have ever travelled started by telling the passengers that they would spend the first two hours of the tour riding Shetland ponies. It was also advisable to pick ones with short front legs as they were easier to sit on when climbing hills. Invariably, they seem to ask me if the concrete markers seen everywhere on the water mains are the gravestones of ponies. One lady was overheard saying to her companion, "Look, these people must be really poor, they have to hang out their washing to dry," presumably meaning that 'they' could not afford a tumble-drier. There is truly 'no'wt as queer as fowk'!

Perhaps the most difficult problem for the tour companies is the directive that every tourist on a particular route must see and visit the same places. This leaves no opportunity to divert to meet the particular wishes of any group – for example to see puffins or ponies – if these are not actually on the published tour route. This stricture is set out because of the ongoing era of litigation and compensation. If some tourists hear that others have been to a different and perhaps more interesting location they are almost bound to sue the cruise operators and demand their money back in the hope of getting a free cruise!

It has been suggested that all tour buses should stop and visit the archaeological excavations at 'Old Scatness', but the vision of five fully-laden 50-seater buses parked at the wrong side of the main road, and 250 mesmerised visitors on that restricted site, leaves me with a sense of dread for the guides who are seen to be responsible for the safety of their charges. Maybe it is time I retired?

Time seems to be at a premium these days, but we did have one unusual holiday in February, 2005, when we went to Funchal in Madeira to join Freddy and Heather Tait at their time-share apartment. Having kitted ourselves out with sunglasses, sun-cream, shorts and the like, we landed in drizzle and this was followed by the worst week of weather the island had encountered for about 20 years. We ended up buying raincoats and sou-westers. Tangles were lying around the seafront swimming pools and there were landslides in the mountains. We did actually manage one afternoon tour in sunshine for a few miles along the coast, but it was not what we, or the locals, had expected. Despite all this, I hasten to add that we thoroughly enjoyed the company, the food and wine.

On our return to Manchester Airport I saw an elderly couple gazing around, obviously completely lost. They had just emerged at 'arrivals', together with what looked like a large proportion of the population of Pakistan. I noticed a uniformed lady standing nearby so suggested that she might tell the old couple on which carousel their luggage would appear. Imagine my surprise when she responded with, "It's a long while since I heard a Lerwick accent." This was none other than Marcelle Wylie, who is on the staff of customs at the airport and whose mother is on the staff of the Shetland Times Bookshop on Commercial Street – truly a small world!

CHAPTER EIGHTEEN

As I was about to say...

I HAVE no doubt that more could be written and that much has been omitted which should have been included, but I do not intend to continue merely to fill spaces.

I find myself rather ashamed that I have reached this stage without mentioning relations other than close family. Compared to Meg, I have remarkably few relations: three nephews – Malcolm, Laurence and Steven, the sons of my half-brother Bay on the Smith side of the family tree, and three first cousins – Jean Smith, Hilary Harmer and Ruth Fletcher from the Campbell side. Apart from Hilary, who now lives with her husband John in Scalloway, the others are in Yorkshire, Devon and Cornwall and, as time passes and the motorways become busier, the once attractive (to me) prospect of a really long drive to the western extremities of Great Britain has waned, so I see more of Hilary than the others. I have to admit that, although I spend a great deal of time writing letters and articles, I am very remiss in not keeping in touch with

With Lerwick Brass Band, Tall Ships, Aberdeen.

these remaining relations, but I am sure that they have realised that for some considerable length of time. The odd email does cross the airwaves, but they are, in my opinion, very impersonal compared with a letter, but much better than nothing.

In September 2008, Meg and I were invited to the 80th birthday party of Douglas Conochie in Aberdeen, and there we met up with some old (in every sense of the word) friends whose names appear throughout these pages. With Jerry Andrew, Dinky Spence, Freddy Tait, myself and Conochie, this represented a real Boys' Brigade reunion, and was a memorable occasion. While in the area we also visited Bertie Laurenson in Elgin, another lifetime friend and colleague from school, Suez Canal Zone and Edinburgh. Shortly after our return home it was the turn of Ian Fraser to join the 80s, so now the

The author, Freddy Tait, Jim Spence, Jerry Andrew and Douglas Conochie (front); 'Boys of the Old Brigade', September 2008.

'three poor mariners' have each managed to reach four score years, and hopefully at least a few more lie ahead, but I am very glad that the answer to that lies beyond our knowledge.

Sadly, the few more years which I mentioned when I wrote the preceeding paragraph were not to be fulfilled for my dear friend and fellow 'mariner' Douglas Conochie. He died in Aberdeen on 14th April, 2009, a few days before we were due to visit him, and while this book was in course of preparation. He is sorely missed and I am sure that, were he still with us, there would have been some very pertinent – and otherwise – comments when he read this, having been party to so much of my life.

As a final footnote, my latest project is in cooperation with a museum in Nova Scotia which is proposing to publish a booklet about the life and death of David Hornell. He was a Canadian airman who was awarded the Victoria Cross and who lies in Lerwick New Cemetery at the Knab. Having provided a fair bit of information about the Shetland end of the story, in the draft copy which I recently received, my name is listed among the acknowledgements as 'Douglas Smith, Shetland – Historian'. Given my earlier struggles and vicissitudes with the subject, it is gratifying to see that my efforts have eventually been recognised, albeit across the Atlantic!

> That was my story, that was my song,
> I've sat at this keyboard rather too long.
> So roll on the ending and then it is done
> and 'Noo Dan' is finished – at long last 'Yun's Yun'!

The two of us, Christmas 2008.